DATE DUE

Underachievers in School:
Issues and Intervention

Underachievers in School: Issues and Intervention

NAVA BUTLER-POR
University of Haifa

JOHN WILEY & SONS
Chichester · New York · Brisbane · Toronto · Singapore

Library of Congress Cataloging-in-Publication Data:

Butler-Por, Nava.
  Underachievers in school.

  Bibliography: p.
  Includes indexes.
  1. Underachievers. 2. Motivation in education.
3. Remedial teaching. 4. Underachievers—Case
studies. I. Title.
LC3969.B87   1987   371.95′6   87–8295

ISBN 0 471 91109 7

British Library Cataloguing in Publication Data:

Butler-Por, Nava
  Underachievers in school : issues and
  intervention.
  1. Education, Elementary 2. Academic
  achievement
  I. Title
  372.12′64   LB1555

ISBN 0 471 91109 7

Typeset by Woodfield Graphics, Fontwell, Arundel, West Sussex.
Printed and bound in Great Britain by Bath Press Ltd, Bath.

I dedicate this book to Nachum, Ruth, David and Eyal

Treat people as if they were
what they ought to be
and
you help them become
what they are capable of being.

Goethe

Contents

Part 1: Identification, Characteristics and Treatment of Underachievers

Part 2: Education of the Underachiever

Foreword

The phenomenon of underachievement is both a baffling and a challenging one—baffling in its complexities and challenging in the significance of its reversal. Some time ago, my colleagues and I wrote:

> Recognition of academic achievement as a serious psychological and social problem reflects the values of a culture which attempts to look beyond performance to potential; maintains a prolonged compulsory system of education; seeks to nurture and develop diversity of abilities within and among individuals, and concerns itself with the maximum development of the individual as well as his contribution to society. (Raph, Goldberg and Passow, 1966).

Our concern at that time was with the intellectually gifted underachiever whom we saw as 'an ubiquitous phenomenon'; who appears in many guises ('lazy, disinterested in school, bored, rebellious, unable to relate to teachers, or having difficulty with one or more subjects'); and was believed not to be using his/her full intellectual potential in meeting the school's academic demands. Quite simply, we defined the underachiever whose performance and scholastic attainment were substantially below their predicted levels. On some basis, the individual's achievement potential is judged to be significantly greater than the actual achievement.

Why this differential exists is the baffling aspect as are the ways and means for reversing this behaviour. The challenge was put well by Gardner in his book *Excellence*:

> Our society cannot achieve greatness unless individuals at many levels of ability accept the need for high standard of performance and strive to achieve those standards within the limits possible for them...the fact that a large number of American boys and girls fail to attain their full development must weigh heavily on our national conscience (Gardner, 1961).

Nava Butler-Por's review of the research literature makes it quite clear that underachievement is a concern to educators and others in many countries, not just in America. In dealing with the cross-national nature of underachievement, she helps our understanding of how the problems are perceived and what is being done and what can be done to help reverse patterns of underachievement.

As when my colleagues and I were conducting our studies of the nature of underachievement and strategies for reversing academic underachievement, there is still not agreement regarding the definition of underachievement, although generally a gap exists between academic achievement and predicted potential, usually based on intelligence or scholastic aptitude test scores. But, since there may be measurement errors in the predictor instruments as well as questions about the validity of the measures, caution should be exercised in evaluating the validity of the predictive measures. There are persons who argue that many factors other than intelligence and scholastic aptitude, many so-called non-intellective factors, affect achievement and, therefore, to expect a one-to-one correlation between achievement and potential is simply unrealistic. And, of course, there are those who believe that all humans, or certainly most humans, are underachievers in the sense that few individuals ever actually realize their full potential. These arguments and reservations are interesting and need to be discussed but they should not deter us from studying the phenomenon and from devising and testing strategies for reversing patterns of underachievement.

Nava Butler-Por provides us with a thoughtful examination of the dynamics and characteristics of academic underachievement based on a thorough review of the research literature, examines and criticizes strategies which have been used to reverse underachieving performance, reports on her effort to develop and evaluate a new model for dealing with underachievement, and synthesizes all of this to provide help for educational practitioners by detailing the implications for teachers and others who are confronted with underachievers. Her discussions are clear and on-target—she bases her proposals for a new intervention model and her suggestions for strategies for reversing underachievement on a blending of research and theory.

Nava Butler-Por's purpose is to provide

> a better understanding of the dynamics of the underachiever and...to provide guidance for teachers in the initiation and implementation of intervention treatment with academic underachievers in their own classes, where the phenomenon presents both a problem and a challenge.

She provides a better understanding of the dynamics of the underachiever through a review of research and theory, thoroughly examining factors which have been associated with academic underachievement—parental and home, personal (e.g. self-concept, locus of control, need achievement, fear of failure, etc.), and school-related. She makes a convincing case for the complexity and dynamic characteristics of academic underachievement and the deleterious consequences which under-achievement has on individuals. Dr Butler-Por then reviews a variety of intervention strategies which have been studied for their effects in overcoming or reversing academic underachievement. Most of these strategies centre on counselling and guidance and/or modifications of curriculum and teaching methods. The studies which my colleagues, Jane Raph and Miriam Goldberg, and I conducted over a period of years are discussed and what we learned from our research presented, noting, quite correctly, that we were not successful in reversing underachievement patterns. Despite our failure, we think we learned a good deal about the phenomenon and its reversal, which Nava Butler-Por has interpreted and integrated into her presentation. What she does very well is to apply research knowledge to helping underachievers overcome their problems.

The application of Glasser's theory of Reality Therapy to the problem of under-achievement provides a basis for the treatment model which Nava Butler-Por presents. In reporting the results of her experimental testing of her model, she builds a case for its value and feasibility. The second part of the book deals with implications for educational practice and deals with a description of the interevention model proposed, the role of teachers in overcoming underachievement, instructional and curricular methods for reducing and preventing underachievement and, finally, the implications for teacher education at both the pre-service and in-service levels.

Educational practitioners and educational researchers concerned with the phenomenon of underachievement will find Nava Butler-Por's book useful, comprehensive, focused and practical. There is no question that she has helped to advance our understanding of the nature of underachievement and the procedures by which it may be reversed.

A. HARRY PASSOW
Jacob H. Schiff Professor of Education Teachers College, Columbia University,
New York, New York 10027

REFERENCES

John Gardner (1961) *Excellence: Can We Be Equal and Excellent Too?* New York: Harper, p. 131
Jane Raph, Miriam Goldberg and A. Harry Passow (1966). *Bright Underachievers*, New York: Teachers College Press, p. 1

Preface and Acknowledgements

This book is organized as a general text for the use of primary school teachers, school counsellors, and teacher training courses at the pre- and in-service levels of education, and university students attending courses in Educational Psychology and Education.

The book consists of two main parts. Part 1 is concerned with the issues related to the problem and treatment of underachievement among children of healthy and normal development, who can be helped by their teachers within the general classroom situation. This part includes a discussion of the prerequisites contributing to the child's motivation for learning, factors influencing the onset of under-achievement and the characteristics associated with it. The final chapter of Part 1 describes and discusses the findings of a study which I conducted with primary school underachievers of both average and superior abilities.

Part 2 is concerned with the implications for educational practice. This section introduces a new intervention programme appropriate for the treatment of under-achievers in class, discusses the teacher's role in helping underachievers and provides diagnostic tools for identification and teaching methods capable of reducing the incidence of underachievement in school. Chapter 8 is concerned with the educational needs of gifted underachievers and girl underachievers. The final chapter discusses the practical implications for pre-service and in-service education of teachers. The references mentioned in the text are presented at the end of the book followed by a bibliography for further reading. A set of appendices referring to the study described in Chapter 4 provides further information on the methodology and findings of the investigation.

The completion of this book would have been impossible without the generous help I have received from all those involved with its progress.

My deep gratitude and appreciation go to Professor Harry Passow of Teachers College, Columbia University for his invaluable advice, continued support and for the writing of the Foreword to this book. I am also most indebted to Ena Abrahams of London University Institute of Education and Professor James Gallagher of University of North Carolina at Chapel Hill for their stimulating and productive comments and valued help and encouragement. I also wish to thank Joan Freeman for her support.

The study reported in Part One was designed as part of my PhD thesis conducted at the University of Wales, University College Cardiff. I wish to acknowledge the kindness and help received and to take this opportunity to thank all those who contributed to its successful completion: Dr Graham Upton for his constructive and devoted Mentorship, Dr John Hawworth of the Department of Mathematical Statistics at University College Cardiff and Dr Tamar Avi-Itzhak of the School of Education at University of Haifa for the thought and time they devoted in assisting me on statistical aspects of the research, and to Ruth Barzilai whose imaginative help with the processing of the data was provided with great dedication.

The study reported in this book would have been impossible to accomplish without the great help, cooperation and support of Dr Joseph Goldstein, the Ministry of Education and Culture Director of Education, Haifa, and all the teachers who participated in the investigation. I also wish to acknowledge the contribution of Aviva Yaar and Lea Binya who provided the material for the learning centres described in Chapter 7.

My thanks are extended to Michael Coombs and Wendy Hudlass at John Wiley's for their good advice and encouragement. To Tamara Beris who typed the manuscript with great care and devotion—my sincere thanks.

Finally, and most of all, I am appreciative and profoundly grateful to my daughter Ruth and my husband Nachum for their sustained interest, help and encouragement.

I greatly value the stimulating concepts that Ruth contributed to model of prere-quisites for learning, described in Chapter 2, and her scholarly advice and assistance in the preparation of the manuscript. My husband, Nachum, provided creative ideas for the graphical presentation of the research and the most important unfailing support which enabled me to complete this book.

Part I: Identification, Characteristics and Treatment of Underachievers

CHAPTER 1

The Problem of Underachievement:
An Introduction

This chapter will introduce the concept, onset and scope of scholastic underachieve-ment. It is suggested that as the patterns of behaviour which are characteristic of underachieving children are enduring, underachievement should be detected in the early stages of the child's primary education before the problem becomes too deeply entrenched to be reversed. It is believed that since underachievement is mainly manifested at school, it should be treated by the teacher within the classroom situa-tion. Finally, the chapter provides an outline of procedures and strategies which should enable teachers to identify underachieving children in their classes.

My earliest insight into the problem of underachievement occurred many years ago, during the opening week of my first job as a supply teacher in a South London primary school. I was told that 'the class was all right, but some children were pretty hopeless'. I was also told that the children were used to working through their arithmetic book and were tested at the end of each week. After receiving the first test papers in long division, most of which were disastrous, I did not know what to do. While I had learnt how to teach arithmetic using the frontal methods prevalent at the time, nothing in my training had prepared me for a class where some children failed because they did not understand the meaning of the zero, some because they had not learned how to carry over numbers from one stage to another, others seemed to have very little understanding of division and would try to divide the smaller number by the larger one, while some children seemed confused and unable to make any sense of the set number work.

I subsequently divided the papers into small groups according to the main errors they revealed, and spent my next lunch breaks working with the children on their own specific difficulties. I soon realized that some of the 'hopeless' children were pretty bright but for different reasons had lost confidence in their ability to cope with their school work. However, I found out that when each child was helped to understand the specific problem in arithmetic that had been holding him back, his progress was not only remarkable, but also quite out of proportion to the effort I invested. As I gained more experience, I met children in every classroom whose performance and achievements gave no indication of their actual abilities. Even when these children revealed their higher potential in one way or another, I, as were most teachers, was often at a loss to help them.

After a period of some years in university teaching, I next came across the problem of children whose school work did no justice to their actual ability, where one might least expect it—in my capacity as adviser to the special classes for highly gifted children in Haifa. While children were selected for the programme on the basis of intelligence and aptitude tests, falling in the top two percentile of their age group, I was frequently approached by teachers who insisted that certain children had been selected by mistake, were not at all gifted, and could not meet the scholastic demands of the class. One of these complaints concerned a second-grade boy who did nothing in class, showed no interest, and was apparently unable to follow learning activities. When I invited the boy for a private talk, he insisted that he did not like learning and was not interested in anything in class. I, myself, might have tended to agree with his teacher had he not, out of the blue, suddenly said: 'I understand why people say that electricity flows, but I don't understand what they mean when they say it is produced.' At this point I began to wonder what, in fact, could be done to help such children. It seemed clear that teachers needed help in understanding the reasons why children who are quite capable of making good progress in school give no indication of their abilities to do so, take no interest in the classroom learning activities, and are thus consistently functioning in school well below their true capabilities. This discrepancy between children's potential for attaining a higher level of achievement and their actual school performance is defined as 'underachievement'. When underachieving patterns of behaviour persist, they create damage both to the individual child who fails to reach full development and to society which is deprived of her possible contribution. However, children are not born underachievers, their school behaviour is acquired (Davis and Rimm, 1985) and fortunately, as my experience has shown, teachers can be very effective in helping underachieving children to fulfil their potential when provided with appropriate methodology on how to help the individual overcome the specific problems which prevent him from enjoying school learning and from attaining the scholastic level of which he is capable.

The aim of this book is to provide teachers and students of education with the tools which can develop both knowledge and attitudes which facilitate understanding of the individual underachiever's needs and to provide effective intervention methods which can be applied and made to work in the classroom.

THE PROBLEM AND SCOPE OF UNDERACHIEVEMENT

While it is generally agreed that realizing the potential of every individual child should be one of the main objectives of education, there are children of all ability levels who, for various reasons, fail to reach their full development and do not attain the scholastic level expected from the majority of their contemporaries. Moreover, among children of exceptionally high intellectual ability, many not only fail to reach the academic level of which they are capable, but quite often their school performance is consistently lower than that of their average ability peers (Terman and Oden, 1947; Burt, 1962; Kellmer-Pringle, 1970; Whitmore, 1980; Gallagher, 1985).

Since the gap between potential and actual school performance seems more dramatic among children of superior intellectual ability in terms of personal and societal loss, efforts to understand and treat the problem have so far mainly been directed to gifted underachievers (Raph, Goldberg and Passow, 1966; Whitmore, 1980; Tannenbaum, 1984; Gallagher, 1985). However, as many teachers have observed, there are children of all ability levels in every classroom whose school work falls well below their capabilities and the expectations of their parents and teachers.

Moreover, the recent important Inner London Education Authority reports on Primary and Secondary Education (The Thomas and Hargreaves Committees, 1984) suggest that underachievement is prevalent in most classroom situations and stress the need for schools to direct attention and effort to enhancing the scholastic achievements of pupils.

While it is impossible to determine the full scope of the problem since underachievement often remains 'hidden', when children, for various reasons which will be discussed in Chapter 2, do not reveal their true abilities, findings from British and American studies provide convincing evidence of great wastage of latent talent in all social classes (Raph, Goldberg and Passow, 1966; Kellmer-Pringle, 1970; Burt, 1975; Tempest, 1974; Gallagher, 1985).

One may well ask why, despite the recognition of the need to reduce the incidences of underachievement in schools so very little progress has been achieved in its remediation? Three main factors seem to provide, at least in part, some explanation.

1. COMPLEXITY OF CAUSATION

Underachievement has many causes which affect each individual differently. Though many characteristics are associated with underachievers (see Chapter 2), the complex and dynamic nature of the individual's problem makes it necessary to understand the specific factors contributing to the individual child's failure to attain the level of achievements that she is capable of. However, many investigations of underachievement concentrated on one or two specific variables assumed to be generally responsible for underachievement. The conflicting results of the effects of these variables on underachievement reported by different researchers were not very helpful for the purpose of the identification and treatment of underachievement (Fink, 1962; Shaw and Alves, 1963; Ziv, 1975).

2. THE ONSET OF UNDERACHIEVEMENT

Since underachievement is more apparent at the secondary level of education, most of the efforts to treat the problem were undertaken at a later stage of the underachiever's schooling, when underachievement patterns of behaviour were already deeply entrenched and difficult to reverse. Because educational failure is cumulative, it is important that underachievement should be detected as early as possible. Underachievement which is present in the earliest school years can be consistent throughout the child's school career if not treated during the child's primary school education (Shaw and McCuen, 1960; Whitmore, 1980).

3. REMEDIAL TREATMENT OF SCHOLASTIC UNDERACHIEVEMENT

Underachievement is manifested in the school, within the classroom situation, and may, in many cases, have its roots in failure to provide appropriate educational experiences in the early school years (Delph and Martinson, 1974; Whitmore, 1980). The school and the teacher have also the greatest potential for successful intervention. However, most of the reported remediation efforts involved counselling to underachievers and their parents by psychologists or counsellors often outside the school and usually without the participation of the teachers involved in the education of the children (Kornrich, 1965; Baymur and Patterson, 1965; Zilli, 1971). Effective intervention should take place within the classroom situation, where underachievement presents both a problem and a challenge.

DEFINITION OF UNDERACHIEVEMENT

Defining what is meant by underachievement is an extremely important but far from simple matter. It is important for teachers to understand what the problem is if they are to attempt to alleviate it. It is not simple since most definitions are based on test results which generally have their pitfalls and in the case of the dynamic nature of underachievement are particularly problematic.

Broadly, underachievement is defined as a large discrepancy between the child's school performance and some manifestation of the child's true ability such as teachers' and parents' observations or achievement, creativity and intelligence measures. For research purposes different methods of identifying underachievers are used. Most studies define underachievers by the large gap between the underachiever's school performance and potential. However, since it is not possible to assess potential accurately, investigators usually define potential on the basis of I.Q. scores while achievement is assessed on the basis of teacher grades or achievement tests (Raph, Goldberg and Passow, 1966). While researchers must attempt to use objective achievement measures, they should consider that not all children at a given age, or even those studying in the same class, are exposed to the same educational experiences. Moreover, since different causes, at different times, affect the child's scholastic behaviour (see Chapter 2) individual test scores should be treated with caution, since they are not necessarily predictors of long-term performance (Thomas Committee Primary Education Report, 1984, 1. 15).

While these factors must be considered by investigators engaged in the study of underachievement, different considerations and approaches should be utilized by teachers who wish to identify underachievers in their own classes. Since many primary schools do not habitually administer intelligence and achievement tests, nor do primary schools in England award school grades, teachers can employ alternative methods of identification which employ the resources available to them within the normal classroom situation. The following section presents an outline of the relevant information which enables the teacher to recognize and detect underachievement in class. The detailed methodology for teacher identification of underachievers is discussed in Chapter 7.

TEACHER IDENTIFICATION OF UNDERACHIEVING PUPILS

Teacher identification procedures should include all the relevant information in any particular educational setting. Our experience suggests that the following methods should identify most underachievers in class.

1. UNDERSTANDING THE BEHAVIOUR AND RECOGNIZING THE CHARACTERISTICS OF UNDERACHIEVERS

It is helpful for teachers to be familiar with the problems and behaviour patterns which are characteristic of underachieving children. While a detailed discussion of these aspects is presented in Chapter 2, some insight at this stage should be useful.

Since the underachiever's poor school achievements are not caused by his inability to do better at school, but are the expression of his conscious or unconscious choice, this 'choice' also determines the behaviours and strategies which he adopts in order to maintain his underachievement. For example, Roth and Meyersberg (1963) found that this 'choice' is expressed in the effort invested in learning. Thus inadequate preparation results in poor skill acquisitions which, in turn, result in poor achievement. As these patterns become deeply entrenched, motivational problems are internalized, affecting the child's general development. This syndrome is characterized by depreciation, lack of clear personal goals and values, vulnerability to disparagement by others, immature relationships and lack of insight about self and others, depression and anxiety (Roth and Meyersberg, 1963).

In addition, characteristics such as inconsistent school work, poor study habits, lack of concentration, daydreaming, hyperactivity, non-completion of assignments and disorganization have often been observed by teachers. It is important to mention that social behaviour may be characterized by obsessive efforts to secure social acceptability by peers, inability to form and maintain social relationships, aggressive behaviour or, in contrast excessive timidity (Rimm, 1984). It is not implied that every child who manifests any of the above mentioned characteristics is an underachiever; however, it is suggested that teachers should detect such behaviour in order to initiate further identification procedures.

2. DIAGNOSTIC TEACHING METHODS

In addition to careful and sensitive observation of children's classroom behaviour, teachers should introduce diagnostic education experiences and teaching methods at the beginning of the school year. These activities are presented and discussed in detail in Chapter 7.

3. COLLECTING RELEVANT DATA

(a) Evaluation of discrepancies

In comparing observed behaviour and characteristics with performance on diagnostic educational experiences, teacher attention should be directed to discrepancies between performance, ability and behaviour (see Chapter 7).

(b) Consulting children's records

Previous reports and school records should be consulted. Notice should be taken of previous teacher evaluation of the child's interest in school work, reading habits, scholastic performance and social behaviour. A consistent drop in a child's school performance of approximately two years indicates that for whatever reasons, this child is underachieving.

(c) Consulting parents

Parents' knowledge and insight is important. Parents should be consulted for possible explanations for children's failure to attain either the school achievements which they managed in previous years, or those that they seem to be capable of on the basis of the information that the diagnostic methods yielded.

(d) Enlisting professional help

In addition to employing the above listed procedures, teachers are advised to seek, when available, further help from the school psychologist, adviser or counsellor, in order to obtain further information as well as discussing the composite picture of the individual underachieving pupil.

By employing the identification procedures discussed above the teacher should gain the relevant information in order to initiate appropriate intervention. However, before we can consider the solutions to the problems of underachieving children, it is important to understand the main factors which are associated with the onset of scholastic underachievement. The following chapter will discuss parental and home variables, personality characteristics and school factors.

CHAPTER 2

The Causes and Characteristics of Scholastic Underachievement

This chapter will attempt to explain the various factors which effect the onset of underachievement. Since the main causes responsible for underachievement are associated with the home and personality characteristics of the underachiever, these will be discussed first. It is believed that though these variables influence the onset of underachievement, the school and the learning situation may contribute to its further development. The discussion of this aspect will, therefore, conclude this chapter. The chapter begins with presenting a model of the prerequisites for 'The Joy in Learning', which when maintained may prevent the onset of underachievement.

This chapter will examine the main causes that are associated with underachievement in order to attempt to answer the question which baffles both teachers and parents—why some children enjoy school, invest effort in their learning and do as well as they are capable of, while others hate school, hardly do any work and consequently their achievements are well below their capabilities.

Attention will be given to the three factors which have been associated in the literature with scholastic underachievement:

(1)   Home and parental variables;
(2)   Personality characteristics;
(3)   School factors

Before asking what went wrong in the home or school of the underachiever, let us first look at what probably went right in the home life of the child who comes to school happy, eager to learn and likely to do as well as his capabilities permit. If we take a broad view of all that has been written from many viewpoints about the child's needs for optimal development, we see that certain basic ideas and processes tend to recur in one form or another (Maslow, 1954; Erikson, 1963; Piaget, 1958; White, 1959; B.L.White, 1985).

Since it is not within our scope to deal with children who are unable to do well at school because of physical or learning disabilities and whose teachers need special training, we shall restrict our discussion to children of at least average physical, intellectual and cognitive characteristics and development. It seems that a healthy adjustment to school depends on factors relating to the child's personality on the one hand and to her motivation on the other. As we watch Mary going to school on her first day happy and eager to do well at school, and John 'with his satchel and shining morning face, creeping like a snail, unwillingly to school' (Shakespeare, *As You Like It*, Act II, Scene 7), we wonder what are the home factors which account for the different school expectations of Mary and John? Now, let us look at the main prerequisites on which a constructive and creative attitude to learning are probably built. In an attempt to answer this question, my daughter, Dr Ruth Arnon, and I constructed a model, based on the theories mentioned above and on our professional experience, of the prerequisites needed for a predisposition to thrive at school.

The model consists of two aspects:

(1) EMOTIONAL and SOCIAL—since the satisfaction of these needs influences the child's healthy development and personality.
(2) MOTIVATION—since the fulfilment of these needs will determine how well the child will do at school.

PREREQUISITES FOR JOY IN LEARNING

1. HOME FACTORS

(a) Social and emotional

1. Basic Trust
—*Parents and environment recognize the child's needs, try to satisfy them, and succeed more or less in doing so.*

Examples
Parents satisfy the child's hunger, provide warmth and love and are consistent in these behaviours. Thus the child is able to internalize the feeling of basic trust which constitutes the foundation on which his confidence in his environment is being built. It is important to emphasize that no harm will be done if occasionally parents are slightly late with the child's meal, or fail to satisfy the child's need perfectly, for some reason or another. It is the environment's general and regular behaviour which matters.

2. Trust in Others
—*Parents and the social environment provide the child with his growing needs and comfort him when he needs it. Their attention and love reinforce the child's feeling that people are to be trusted.*

Examples
The consistent relief of the child's discomfort accompanied by love and interest in all that he does enables him to acquire the sense of permanency in his security and to extend his concept that others around him are trustworthy.

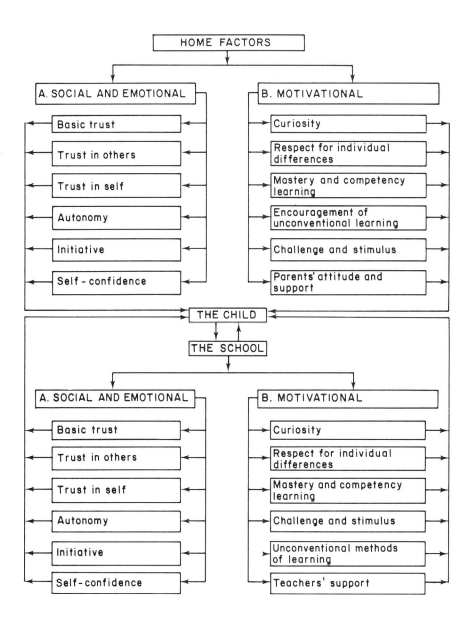

Figure 2.1   Prerequisites for joy in learning.

3. Trust in Self
—Parents and the social environment respond with interest and joy to the child's activities. Help is provided when needed. Safe but unrestricted environment is provided. This encourages new learning and acquisition of skills. Parents express delight with the child's new achievements. Trust in self is thus being built.

Examples
The child manages, perhaps accidentally, to use a spoon to eat her porridge. Her mother is delighted and calls everybody in the house to see it. This enthusiasm enhances the child's confidence in herself and she proceeds in trying again and again. Her successes, received with delight, reinforce her notion that she can succeed when she tries.

4. Autonomy
—Parents are willing and able to foster the child's independence and autonomy in his ventures to explore his world, while maintaining a safe and secure physical and emotional environment.

Examples
The child insists on finding out how to operate a complicated new mechanical device at home. The parents do not discourage her, nor do they rush to help her when she fails, rather she is encouraged to try again. Thus the parents convey emotional security and reinforce the concept that independence is legitimate.

5. Initiative
—Parents and family are willing to let the child discover and explore his environment and to be enthusiastic about and complimentary of the child's adventurous enterprises.

Examples
The child takes the initiative to organize some of his friends into 'a tree-climbing club'. Since there are good trees to climb in his garden he invites his friends over to start the club's activities. Parents do no object, despite the responsibility involved, but they unobtrusively keep 'a watching eye'.

6. Self-confidence
—Parents provide the child with affirmation that the child is capable, is growing vis-à-vis herself, that she is not compared with others. Not saying, for example, that your brother, Johnny, was even better than you at doing a particular activity when he was your age.

Examples
Every healthy child has the capacity for experiencing the achievement of acquiring various motor skills, like sitting, walking, climbing, etc. The thrill the child derives from learning serves to enhance her self confidence and stimulate her to practise and improve her newly acquired skill. The role of the interested adult observer, that of reinforcing the joy of accomplishment, is most significant (B.L.White, 1985).

(B) Motivational

1. Curiosity
—*Parents recognize the child's need to satisfy his curiosity in his world and all its wonders. Parents encourage the child to explore and provide opportunities and stimulation capable of satisfying his curiosity. The reinforcement that follows the child's inquiry and subsequent new learning, rewards him and motivates him for further learning. This process, when consistent, is internalized by the child and contributes to his healthy personality.*

Examples
The child shows curiosity in how the batter becomes a cake. Parents share the activity with the child and let him bake his own cake, risking the 'fall' of mother's cake by opening the oven.

2. Awareness and respect for individual interests
—*Parents recognize and accept the child's individuality in terms of her need to develop her own interests.*

Examples
Parents do not discourage their daughter's interest in cars and mechanical toys and do not keep coaxing her to play with her dolls.

3. Mastery and competency learning
—*Parents provide the child with ample opportunities to try out things for herself. The child's social environment provides her with continuous feedback that she can do things for herself. The child's actual competence and sense of competence and effective behaviour towards others, are secured from her accumulated experiences of success (White, 1959). The home environment provides tasks that the child can master, opportunities to accomplish more and more over time, and supplies the child with continuous information about her efforts which enables the child to assess and develop her competence. Parents' ample linguistic input supplies the child with the information to confirm her ability.*

Examples
The child has learnt to categorize her library books according to topics, to arrange them in order of those she liked best and to paint a symbol for each topic. She has invested a lot of effort in thinking it out and accomplishing the task which she herself chose to do. When finished, she shows it to her brother and asks him if he thinks it is all right. He tells her it is wonderful and promptly summons all people who are in the house to see it. The child is complimented on her achievement and ideas with great enthusiasm by all present. Such behaviours reinforce the child's sense of competence.

14

4. *Encouragement of unconventional ideas and methods of learning*
—*Parents accept and encourage the child's creativity and unusual ideas and unconventional methods of accomplishing tasks and solving the everyday problems encountered by him. Parents seek to provide the child with tasks relating to his individual tastes.*

Examples
The child is a 'collector'. He has started a collection of ordinary household corks. Though his parents think this is not a worthwhile idea, they contribute to his collection and compliment him on the unusual way he has arranged them and congratulate him on the unconventional method of his categorization and new ideas of usage of the corks. The parents' response is most important in encouraging the child to take the 'risk' of venturing out with new ideas.

5. *Challenge and stimulus*
—*Parents and environment provide the child with interesting and different tasks to accomplish. Parents provide ample input of challenging and stimulating things for the child to do and take an interest in. Parents refrain as far as possible from normative evaluation of the child's achievements. Rather, emphasis is placed on the child's interest and effort invested. These socialization patterns reinforce the child's belief that effort and interest are more important than sheer ability and rewards. Thus parents provide the required prerequisites to enter school with the expectation that learning will be exciting.*

Examples
Parents encourage the child to expand her interests by providing challenging things to do and sharing them with the child. A lively and sincere interest in the child's world with attempts to broaden and deepen the child's thinking is important as it develops her capacity and enjoyment of coping with challenge.

6. *Parents' attitudes and family support*
—*Parents have positive attitudes for achievement, yet accept the child's individual abilities, expect him to do as well as these abilities enable him, accept with respect his achievements, but do not put pressures on him to accomplish the things he is not ready for or capable of. Parents provide support and help, share the child's*

Examples
One child in the family is less bright than his brother and sister. The parents help him to develop further, encourage and praise him when he has accomplished a new task or has made progress in learning new skills, convey to him that he is able to do things, but are careful not to pressurize him by comparing him to his brother and

enthusiasm and comfort him when things go wrong: providing social guidance with respect to the child's social relations, yet conveying to the child that he is special to them, just as other people are special to those in the world who care about them (B.L.White, 1985).

sister. Parents should try to find the uniqueness in him and share these feelings enthusiastically with the whole family.

In order to succeed, parents need to create a stable home climate which will enable the child to develop fully. This can be achieved if members of the family also receive support from each other.

It is clear that these emotional, social and motivational prerequsities are interdependent and should constitute a process to be continued when the child enters school, in order to ensure that the joy in learning is carried on and further developed in school. Indeed, when we examine each aspect discussed above, we realize that these conditions should and can be fulfilled by the school, when translated by the classroom teacher into establishing a comfortable and supportive class climate, respecting individual needs and the uniqueness of each child, creating a good relationship with every child and introducing the appropriate teaching methods capable of fulfilling the aspects discussed above. This aspect and the operational methodology will be developed later on. Thus the school can maintain and develop the child's joy for learning which is the basis for the motivation of good school achievements and further accomplishments.

CAUSES FOR UNDERACHIEVEMENT

1. HOME AND FAMILY FACTORS

The question that must now be asked is: what can go wrong in the family which prevents its members from satisfying the child's needs which were discussed above, and thus impeding his healthy development and contributing to the onset of underachievement?

We shall attempt to examine the various home factors while emphasizing that these affect each individual child differently. The following example may probably illustrate the problematic nature of the home's influence on the child's underachievement.

HOSTILITY, as a result of denial of basic needs

John's parents divorced when he was two years old. His mother, a fairly intelligent woman, brought him up. His father was of a much higher intellectual level, very involved with his academic career. He tried to form a good relationship with his son, but his visits to him were too sporadic and he spent too little time with him to be able to form a deeper attachment. As a young child John learnt that he could not rely on his parents when he most needed them. His mother came home late from work, his father he hardly saw. It is obvious that John could not acquire trust in others, or in himself, as he was deprived of the consistent and caring satisfaction of his needs from his parents. As he grew a little older, being a naturally lively and intelligent boy he began exploring his world and trying to do new things. However, he never received enthusiastic reinforcement when he most needed it from his parents, or from any substitute caring adult, since the girl who looked after him was busy with the household chores and was not really interested in John. Thus the joy of learning was not really experienced by him. He became very hostile to both his parents and learnt to manipulate them, by extracting presents from them. The mother, who felt continuously very guilty towards him, became very vulnerable to his wishes, but was unable to give him the guidance he needed. When he started school, being quite intelligent he tried to fool his teacher by lies and manipulation into thinking that he was making good progress at school. When things started going wrong, the teacher approached his mother, telling her that the boy was often truant and did not work at all. The mother did not believe her and always defended John. She said that he was very bright and most interested in school. When he was eight years old, his new teacher began to work seriously on his underachievement by trying to provide some of the needs denied him in early childhood. The teacher provided John with consistent attention and interest, sharing his interests with him, sharing his choice of weekly tasks and providing consistent feedback and reinforcement on their completion, conveying to him that he was special. (This model of intervention will be discussed in detail in Chapter 5.

When we attempt to understand the reasons and motives for the child's underachieving behaviour, we recognize the role that his hostility to his parents played. This aspect was also experienced by others (Shaw and Grubb, 1958) and discussed fully by Raph, Goldberg and Passow (1966).

It is important that teachers can share the child's problem with the parents, in order to work together first on the urgent problems of the child. Manipulative behaviour, as in John's case, has frequently been shown to be associated with underachievement (Davis and Rimm, 1985). Hostility can also be created for different reasons such as sibling jealousy, feeling of deprivation, threat and excessive pressure.

(a) Excessive parental pressure

When children feel continuous and excessive parental pressure to attain high achievements they think they cannot reach, they are not able to stand up to the constant pressure and achieve what they feel their parents expect of them. This feeling may discourage them from attempting to even try to do well. When they begin school they perceive the new situation as a threat and choose to avoid it by doing nothing at all or as little work as they can get away with. Often parents are not aware of their own behaviour and could, if the teacher approached them, try to change it while the teacher worked with the child on his underachievement.

In other cases the pressure on the child may be the result of either both or one of the parents' deep frustration caused by their own feeling of inadequate self-realization or other reasons. Their behaviour in such cases may be much more difficult to change (Wellington and Wellington, 1963; Raph, Goldberg and Passow, 1966).

(b) Parental expectations

When parents' expectations are unrealistically too high for the child's ability, the child may become discouraged and fears to disappoint them. This fear of failure, which will be discussed in the next section, may drive the child to avoid failure by refraining from trying or saying new things, and from wishing to face any challenge whatsoever. When the child starts school, these feelings carry on and are expressed in underachieving behaviour. When parents' expectations are too low the child is not urged to undertake tasks at home which the parents do not expect her to fulfil. Thus her perception of herself will tend to match that of her parents with no relationship to her actual ability. When she starts school, she will tend to go on fulfilling the low expectations of her parents, unless she is fortunate enough to meet the teacher who will recognize that she can do much better and try to help her attain the achievements that her ability permits. It is important that the teacher shares her higher expectations with the parents.

(c) Parental attitudes

The role of parents' attitudes and values is very important in shaping the child's attitude to learning. When the parents' attitudes and values are inconsistent and not clear to the child, it is very difficult for him to internalize them. When either one or both of the parents express negative attitudes to learning and academic accomplishments and persist with these attitudes when the child begins school, he carries these attitudes with him to school. It parents show no interest in the child's school progress and the school's activities, the child has no real incentive to work hard, take an interest in school and function according to his capabilities (Ziv, 1975). The child becomes an underachiever. It is very important that teachers understand these causes for underachievement outside the school (Gallagher, 1985).

(d) Home climate and support

The cognitive functioning of adult or child is a very much dependent on his emotional stability and well-being. A child may be deprived of the emotional and social prerequisites for joy in learning during her early childhood in an unhappy home climate due to a parent's illness or absence from home, or to a poor relationship between parents. These factors and the tension it creates at home have a very serious effect on the child's healthy development and her adjustment to school life. They may have a detrimental effect on the development of those variables of her personality which will determine her ability and motivation to do well in school. These personality characteristics will be discussed in the next section.

2. PERSONALITY CHARACTERISTICS

Since parents and families differ in their views of what a good home is and what the needs of their growing children are, we cannot expect all children to respond to the lack of fulfilment of their needs in the same manner. The prerequisites for healthy development, as described above, tell us what should be the motivational outcomes for children who have enjoyed the advantages of a supportive and warm home, with loving parents who are interested in their daily achievements and encourage further accomplishments, and in contrast, what happens to children who are not so fortunate. Children who responded with underachieving behaviours were characterized, as many observed, by low self-image, blaming bad luck for their failures, lacking the ability to set realistic goals and lacking self-discipline (Zilli, 1971). My study of primary school underachievers (to be discussed in Chapter 4) has discovered that underachieving children, just like all children, differ from each other not only in their home background, but also in their own way of coping with their problems. Since teachers are likely to meet underachieving children with different personality characteristics, it is important that they become familiar with these traits, so that they will be able to recognize children's behaviour which may be the result of these characteristics, which usually reflect the lack of satisfaction of some important needs at home and which, when consistent, may be manifested in underachieving behaviour.

If we look back at our model of prerequisites for 'Joy in Learning' in the previous section, we conclude that it is not surprising that children who do not receive positive reinforcement for their efforts and who are constantly criticized for their poor achievements, see themselves as their environment perceives them—in a very poor light. These children often develop a low image of themselves, which may mask their actual capabilities and therefore will probably lead eventually to school performance which is well below actual ability. The dynamics of these personality characteristics need further discussion.

(a) Self-concept

The self-concept of the child is like the self reflected in a looking-glass which is shaped by all the positive and negative reflections received from meaningful individuals in the child's environment (Cooley's theory, in Ziv, 1975). Therefore the child perceives both his successes and his failures through this looking-glass, which actually shows him how his parents and family perceive them. When the child begins school he brings this picture of himself with him. A child who internalized mostly negative responses from the people who were most important to him in the family during his early childhood, formed a low self-concept and, quite understandably, had no reason to expect that he would be able to thrive at school, master new skills, fulfil challenging tasks and believe that his efforts might help him overcome school difficulties (Raph, Goldberg and Passow, 1966; Fink, 1962; Shaw and Alves, 1963; Gallagher, 1985).

Since the young child mainly reflects his parents' views, he may also be an underachiever with a high self-concept, if his parents have a high opinion of him but did not value school and had a low attitude to school. This has been found in the case of highly gifted underachievers (Ziv, 1975). The following examples illustrate effects of the underachiever's self-concept on his school work.

AN UNDERACHIEVER WITH A HIGH SELF-CONCEPT

Johnny, a fourth-grade junior child with an I.Q. in the upper 5 per cent of his class, was always in trouble at school. He kept disrupting the lessons, interfered with other children, never completed assignments and showed no interest in the school activities. His teachers assumed that his behaviour was the result of his frustration because he was too 'dim' for his class. When his parents were consulted, they seemed surprised and assured the teacher that Johnny was very bright, citing various advanced books that he had read at home, hinting that his activities at home were much more important than school as he attended a computer club, played the violin and belonged to a rowing club. When the teacher discussed the child with me, it turned out that he was indeed very bright but agreed with his parents that no effort should be invested at school as it was not important to him. The teacher accepted the challenge to work with the child and his parents on changing Johnny's underachieving behaviour and gaining his involvement in the class activities. It was not easy, but the teacher's high motivation helped!

AN UNDERACHIEVER WITH A LOW SELF-CONCEPT

Ann, a third-grade primary pupil with an average I.Q. for her class, was a very quiet girl. At school she seemed to be attentive, tried to do her school work, but hardly ever completed school assignments. Her teacher was under the impression that she could do better but had no faith in her ability to successfully accomplish more complex tasks. When urged to try, she usually answered 'it's no good, I could not do it'. When her parents were consulted they confirmed the child's low perception of herself, adding that she was always slow. As mentioned above, she was far from slow, but was unfortunate in having a much brighter, older sister, to whom, it appeared, she was always being compared. In Ann's case, the work was much easier. She responded with delight to the teacher's attention and praise for her effort and progress. (The method is described in detail in Chapter 5).

The examples above emphasize the important role that children play in changing their own scholastic achievements. It is clear that their ability to understand that their situation is not the result of 'bad luck' and that indeed they are able to change their school performance is important (Mitchell and Piatkowska, 1974). This factor, known as locus of control, is of significance for teachers who wish to help their children attain the achievements which their capabilities permit.

(b) Locus of control

The underachiever has often been described as a pupil who blames others and 'bad luck' for his school problems. He also feels that he cannot control his school situation (Shaw and Black, 1960; Raph, Goldberg and Passow, 1966; Whitmore, 1980).

The personality variable of locus of control was perceived by Rotter (1954) as a motivational factor, and is of particular relevance to understanding the behaviour of the underachiever. When the child believes that things that happen to her are the result of her own behaviour and are, therefore, controlled by her, she is characterized by internal locus of control. When a child attributes all that happens to him to chance, bad luck and other factors that he is unable to control he is characterized by external locus of control, which is also a characteristic of many underachievers. When we look at our motivational prerequisites for building the child's confidence in himself, convincing him that he can do things for himself and do them well if he invests sufficient effort, we can understand the importance of understanding this variable to teachers who have been shown in my study and others (Bar Tal and Zohar, 1977) as very capable of shifting the child's external locus of control to an internal one and thus assuming responsibility for working towards improving his school achievements (Whitmore, 1980; Clizbe *et al.*, 1980).

The following example serves to illustrate this important motivational factor:

Edna, a fifth-grade primary school pupil, an underachiever of average intelligence compared to her class peers, was believed by her teacher to be able to do much better. Her school achievements were very poor indeed, no tasks were ever completed, her work was careless and untidy and her attitude to school and peers was very negative. She always complained to her teacher that her neighbours in class interfered with her work, that her brother tore up her books, that her previous teachers always wanted her to fail, etc. She believed firmly that no effort could ever improve her situation because everybody was against her, and anyhow she always had bad luck. When her teacher was told that she had been selected for intervention, she herself seemed dubious. However, after some work on Edna's background, she gained some insight into the reasons for the child's perception of herself and was ready to accept the challenge. It transpired that Edna had a charming invalid older brother who attracted her parents' full attention and love. Her parents had perceived Edna, since babyhood, as an ugly nuisance and neglected her completely. Moreover, she was always blamed for everything that happened at home and persistently told that she just could not do anything right. It was no wonder that she had no expectations of doing well at school and no wish to invest any effort, either in learning or in making friends. The pattern of being blamed for everything at home was conveniently reversed to blame her class mates and brother for her failures in school. The gradual change in the child's accomplishment and attitudes provided both the teacher and Edna with very important confirmation that the child can indeed see the relationship between her behaviour and her results and can begin to assume responsibility for planning her school work and setting her goals for the desired achievements.

So far we have seen that the underachiever has often been described as a child who could do better work if he would only try, or as one who lacks motivation for learning. Statements of this nature, which are frequently made by teachers in relation to some of their pupils, are often followed by advice that the child should invest more effort in, and devote more time to his school work. This belief, often shared by parents and teachers, that if only the child would try harder, her scholastic problems could be solved, does not explain why some children appear to be motivated at school, whereas others fail to respond to the efforts of their teachers and parents to motivate them to improve their school performance. To understand it, we must consider the child's whole growth, discussed in the previous section. Our last example illustrated the damage caused by denying a growing child practically all the basic needs required for a healthy development. It is no wonder that the child blamed her environment for her failure. The need to strengthen the child's confidence in himself as a person who is able to take responsibility for his actions and to realize that the results are caused by his actions is a most important function of parents' behaviour and expectations.

The following example illustrates this point:

The other day on the beach, my son and I witnessed the following scene: A mother of a five-year-old boy was forcing food into her overweight child, who refused to eat. She was continuously fussing over him telling him what he liked to eat and do. The boy, unsuccessfully, tried to get away to play. Sometime later they prepared to leave and the mother informed her son that someone had stolen his sand spoon. He asked who did it and she replied: 'another child', saying that there are also small thieves adding: 'You will not be a small thief'. The child replied: 'No, I shall be a big thief!'.

It is important to note that there were no other children in sight. This mother, though not denying the child food or attention, was nevertheless denying him the opportunity to grow into an independent child capable and motivated to solve his problems. Moreover, she was setting the child an example of her own external locus of control. In this case, for example, she should have suggested to the child that he look for the spoon, which was obviously buried in the sand. This child, who already showed signs of rebelling by suggesting that he would become 'a big thief' may well become an underachiever at school and need a great deal of help from the teacher in order to overcome his problems before he can begin to function better at school. This pattern was also explained by a lack of internal need to attain high achievements which must be conveyed to the child by parents' attitudes to achievements through socialization and child-rearing patterns. However, as we shall see, this 'need achievement' (McClelland *et al.*, 1953), in the case of underachievers, is more complicated (Shaw, 1961; Simon and Bibb, 1974) and can better be understood when it is linked to the child's fear of failure (Atkinson and Raynor, 1974). Since teachers can help the child to overcome some of these problems, it is important to discuss these characteristics in greater detail.

(c) Need achievement and fear of failure

The problematic effect of these motivational characteristics is illustrated clearly in the following example:

Tommy, an intelligent fourth-grade primary pupil, (placed in the top 10 per cent of his peers on standardized aptitude tests) was referred to me by his teacher, as a very difficult boy. She did not believe that he was bright since he always cried in class, especially when he was asked to do any school work. When asked to select any topic that interested him, he invariably said that he could not do any work in school, cried and said he could only do it at home. On the teacher's suggestion that he should work with a friend, he answered that nobody wanted to work with him and added that he wouldn't understand anyhow. The teacher was at a loss. It transpired that Tommy had a very bright and successful (according to the parents) sister in a different school who was always set as an example to him. His parents were professional people, highly achievement-oriented, who claimed on the one hand that Tommy was very bright and could attain high achievements but the school underrated him, while on the other hand, they managed to inculcate in Tommy that failure was to be avoided by all means, and encouraged him to bring all his school work home where it was completed by the parents. It was quite clear that the child had been receiving very muddled messages from his parents. The dominant one, however, was quite clear—failure is bad, it must be avoided! His frustration at school was expressed by crying and avoidance action. When this very complicated pattern was eventually understood, the teacher had to work very patiently with Tommy, building his confidence and providing him with a variety of success experiences. Work with the parents then followed.

Tommy's case is not uncommon among underachievers whose home environment 'encourages' them to choose not to cope with school and friends, and it indicates that while the motive to achieve success is present in some form or another in every child, in some children the possibility of failure presents too great a threat, preventing them from trying to cope with learning experiences which are appropriate for their capabilities. This situation presents a conflict between their need and ability to achieve and their great fear of failing. They often resolve this situation by selecting learning tasks which are far too easy for them or assignments which are too difficult for most of the class members and thus the possibility of failure does not constitute a threat (Atkinson, 1958; Atkinson and Raynor, 1974). When this pattern of behaviour persists, it usually leads to underachievement.

(d) Need affiliation

The situation described above can become even more aggravating when children have social needs which they do not know how to fulfil. Tommy, for example, could not satisfy his need for affiliation with friends in class. Since that particular class had a very favourable attitude to learning and scholastic achievements, his reluctance to undertake serious school work may have stemmed from his fear of failure while other pupils were succeeding. This group climate must have further encouraged Tommy to adopt avoidance behaviour which, unfortunately, was reinforced by his parents. It was also of no help in securing friends, which for him, as for all children with high need affiliation, was most important (Schneider, 1977).

(e) Fear of success

As we have seen above, underachievement may be the result of the child's inability to fulfil conflicting needs. In many cases, mostly girls, the social and cultural demands conflict seriously with their ability and need to attain high achievements. The social conflict may create fear of success in women (Horner, 1968), which may also interfere with the attainment of scholastic achievements. The feeling of ambivalence to academic success has been found among middle-class and professional parents and schools, as well as in educational disadvantaged and differently cultured environments (Butler and Nisan, 1975). While fear of success is mainly felt by adolescent girls who begin to identify with their role in adult society, it was found that gifted girls perceived scholastic success as threatening to their feminine status and associated success with rejection by society much earlier—during their primary school education (Butler-Por, 1982). Thus fear of success for girls can result in conscious or subconscious depression of motivation for scholastic success and leads to underachievement.

The following example is not unusual:

Debra, a bright fifth grade primary school girl, attending a middle-class school, attracted the teacher's attention by what seemed to her the very great gap between her ability and her school achievement. The teacher noticed that the girl's verbal expression, her imaginative and creative ideas and understanding of concepts, seemed much higher that her written work, her interest and participation in class tasks and her motivation to accomplish school assignments. When she discussed her impression with Debra, the girl denied her ability, adding that anyhow learning was not important for girls and that it had done no good to her mother. Baffled, the teacher arranged to meet her mother, who was divorced, and held a high academic position. The mother insisted that the teacher was mistaken in thinking that Debra could do better. She was not at all bright. It transpired that the mother had conveyed to Debra that her academic success had ruined her marriage. After a great deal of persuasion the mother agreed to enrol the child in an enrichment course for gifted children. The teacher and Debra were delighted.

Ironically, the following year, the teacher thought that she had made a mistake, that the girl was not an underachiever, but simply worked according to her abilities. Sadly, the child's deep fear of success won. Her conflict was too deep to permit her to fulfil her high potential.

It is obvious that a great deal of work needs to be done to combat the negative societal and cultural influences on the female school population in order to reduce this kind of underachievement amongst them (Hitchfield, 1973; Butler and Nisan, 1975; Butler-Por, 1985).

Fortunately despite unfortunate home factors, the teacher is able to fulfil some of the needs that have not been satisfied at home, and thus help the child to overcome the effects of some of the personality characteristics that have interfered with the ability to function at school according to ability. In the following section, the important role of school in reinforcing or reducing underachievement will be considered.

3. SCHOOL FACTORS

Since scholastic underachievement is mainly a school problem, efforts to deal with the problem should relate to the school situation. This section will outline the main factors within the school which may contribute to the development or prevention of underachievement.

As the school is the only place which at one time or another embraces nearly the whole population, it also has the greatest potential for working towards the detection and prevention of underachievement (Moulin, 1970). The evidence from an important recent English study has demonstrated that the school plays a significant role in enhancing the academic development of its pupils, even when the pupils initially have low achievements and behaviour problems (Rutter *et al.*, 1979). Since underachievement is widespread and concerns the school population of all ages (Thomas and Hargreave Reports, 1984), it seems important to understand the factors within the school situation that are conducive to the onset of the problem. It seems that three main aspects are important: (Frankel, 1960; Tannenbaum, 1962; Newsom, 1963; Rutter *et al.*, 1979; Whitmore, 1980; Pilling and Pringle, 1978).

(a)   Attitudinal factors.
(b)   Curriculum and teaching methods.
(c)   Teacher variables.

It is interesting that these three areas are interdependent, relating directly to the fulfilment of the child's basic needs in school. When we consider the prerequisites needed to develop the joy for learning that the home should provide, we can perceive that although the socialization in the family sets the stage for the healthy development of the child, the teacher has an important role in fulfilling these needs within the learning situation, so that the child can benefit from the educational experience provided by the school. It is believed that an understanding of these needs has a practical value for teachers, since it can help in shaping the teacher's attitude to individual needs, selecting appropriate curriculum experiences and teaching methods, and encouraging the creation of personal and peer interactions which should motivate the child to maximize her efforts towards enjoying learning for its own sake. Though individual differences and difficulties will account for uneven response and progress of some children, it provides the teacher with the tools and motivation to either undo the harm done by the home, as discussed in section one, or to reinforce the sound basis of the home and to develop the child's desire to enhance her achievements.

THE ROLE OF THE SCHOOL

In order to understand this role of the school, let us reconsider our original model, in terms of the classroom situation (see Figure 2.1).

PREREQUISITES FOR JOY IN LEARNING

(a) Social and emotional

(i) Basic trust

The child's basic trust in his home environment is extended to his new school environment, which constitutes the basic foundation on which his attitude to all school experiences can be built. The teacher's welcoming attitude on the first day of school is essential. It should be emphasized that as far as the child is concerned, each new school year is a fresh beginning. Thus the teacher's behaviour on this day is critical. It can reinforce negative attitudes or create new hopes for a better and more satisfying school life. While Chapter 7 will discuss in detail the methods and teacher strategies which have been found effective in creating positive attitudes to school, the following example illustrates the interdependent roles of school attitudes, curriculum and teaching methods and teacher behaviour in combating underachievement:

Jerry, the youngest child of a family of five older brothers and sisters, who treated him as a 'weakling', was brought up by his doting and overprotective grandmother. As she brought him to my reception class on the first day of school, he clung to her hand and cried, entering the classroom late. The children were already active in preparing models and pictures of their holiday experiences. Jerry was at a loss since his home life failed to enhance his confidence, and did not lead him to expect the school to be a secure and trusting environment. I suggested to Jerry that he help in preparing a model of one of my experiences during the holiday. It was interesting to note that when we had finished, Jerry asked me to help him complete a picture of one of his experiences during the holidays which I willingly agreed to do. The activities of the day, which included children's discussion and illustration of their holiday experiences, a teacher's survey of the things which would be learnt and how they would be done, were both reassuring and exciting for Jerry. At the end of the school day Jerry could feel that his negative attitudes to the new school environment were not justified. However, his insecurity persisted for some time. For example, for the following few weeks, Jerry entered the class, a little late, clinging to his grandmother's hand saying: 'Please may I stop by you?'. However, one day, he said simply as he entered: 'I am going to my place!'. Gradually, through curriculum work that he found he could cope with, by using teaching methods that enabled him to receive daily confirmation from me that he was making progress and ample encouragement for undertaking new exciting tasks, Jerry's attitude to school changed, facilitating enjoyment of learning and desire to attain good school achievements.

This example emphasizes the need for the teacher to create a secure classroom environment, emotionally and socially, in which every child can feel safe to express feelings of fear and insecurity, knowing that neither the teacher nor the classmates will sneer or laugh. Only then can the child begin to enjoy the cognitive experiences provided and have a good chance to thrive in school.

(ii) Trust in others

A classroom climate which enables the child to perceive her peers and her teachers as trustworthy is the creation of the teacher. A teacher who demonstrates his respect for each individual child introduces teaching strategies which help him become aware of each child's needs and a flexible approach to the curriculum which makes it possible for the individual child to express his specific needs, weaknesses and strengths. For example, during individual and independent work, systematic time allocation should be made for separate discussion with each child on her school and home interests, on her evaluation of her work, on her likes and dislikes at school and on an assessment of her social situation. Methodical notes of these discussions should be kept which will enable the teacher to get to know the child, to establish a good trusting relationship with each child and to identify underachieving children or those at risk of becoming so. These practices transfer the teacher's trust of all the pupils to each individual child. The awareness that each child and his work is worthy of the teacher's attention reinforces the child's trust in others, or helps develop it in him if it was not possible for him to acquire this trust during his early childhood at home.

(iii) Trust in self

Children who arrive at school with inadequate trust in themselves as a result of parents' failure to fulfil the basic needs required for establishing confidence in oneself, without which new skills and accomplishments cannot be mastered, cannot be expected to develop confidence in themselves in school without appropriate help from the teacher. These children begin their school career as underachievers and will remain so unless intervention commences immediately. However, when it is detected early, it is possible to reverse their situation. The teacher in these cases has an important role to play in initiating individual mastery learning. The child should be given tasks that he can accomplish and frequent opportunities to do more and more over time, thus being able to acquire competence in new skills. It is important to provide the child with the information, through personal communication with the teacher, to assess his progress, experience success and develop further competence. The child should be involved in selecting tasks and regulating his progress. Thus the child can internalize trust and confidence in himself and develop motivation for attaining higher achievements. It is important to emphasize that the child's progress can be uneven, as are all remediation processes. The teacher should take care not to convey disappointment to the child during the less productive periods. Gallagher describes the underachiever's progress most poignantly:

> The dance of the underachiever can be described symbolically as three steps forward, two steps back and one step sideways—pause for effect. (Gallagher, 1985, p. 425).

However, when the teacher believes in the underachiever's ability to change and progress, the child does not lose trust in himself and results can eventually be very rewarding.

It is important to stress that care must be taken to reinforce each child's trust in self. Sometimes, there is the temptation to 'dampen' a child's very demonstrative self-confidence by ignoring or using ironical comments, such as 'You always know all the answers, don't you?' or something similar. Such teacher behaviour can cause damage and has been known to contribute to the onset of underachievement behaviour, when an outgoing and confident child realizes that he must hide his knowledge and enthusiasm in class. Though one can understand the teacher's impatience, such children can be channelled to accepting responsibility for projects or duties in class and should be encouraged and given praise for their efforts.

(iv) Autonomy and initiative

A rigid, formal and inflexible curriculum, utilizing teaching methods which do not allow the child to exercise his need for autonomy and develop the need for practising initiative can contribute to reinforcing or developing underachieving behaviour. For example, children who have been deprived of these needs during early childhood will not be able to exercise autonomy in learning and initiative in choice of developing areas of interests and methods of learning most suited to their temperament and personality. When they come to school they will tend to expect the teacher to tell them exactly what to do. If the teacher uses only a structured curriculum and formal methods of teaching, expecting all class members to follow the same curriculum material at the same time, these children will have no chance of developing autonomous behaviour and exercising initiative, characteristics without which they will not be able to discover their abilities and extend their world of experiences. For potentially bright children, their practised underachieving behaviour can be a life sentence.

In contrast, for children who were socialized into autonomous behaviour and encouraged at home to exercise initiative, a restrictive classroom situation can be most frustrating. When it persists over time, it will probably encourage underachieving behaviour. On the other hand, when the curriculum is flexible, allowing for individual differences and spontaneous enrichment based on children's extended interests, children will be encouraged to develop and exercise initiative in choice of material and make a personal contribution to the class.

Imaginative and flexible teaching methods, and respect for unconventional ideas are needed for the development of creativity. Classroom fulfilment of these needs provides continuous channels of communication which will help children towards gaining self-perception of competency—an important factor in motivation to achieve.

(b) Motivation

(i) Curiosity

All children are curious. They have an inborn need to find out how things work and to understand the world around them. These needs to discover, understand and learn constitute a strong intrinsic motivational force in the child's learning. A child who has been encouraged to fulfil this need at home looks forward to its fulfilment at school. The following description written by Inbal, aged 7, in her diary as a song, illustrates this point:

'To Learn the Bible'.
Today I am so happy
Today I am going to learn
How the world was created.
How the world was chaos,
And by God's hand changed.
I shall start to study diligently,
I shall be an industrious pupil.
Now I am so happy—
I shall learn how things began.

Three weeks later, Inbal wrote in her diary:

To learn the Bible is awful,
All the time to listen
All the time to write a.nd hear
A story I think did not happen.
O' how terrible to learn everything by heart.
To read it to the teacher, nicely.
I wish the Bible will not be taught—
For each story to be repeated twice!

For Inbal, the teacher succeeded in killing her initial curiosity in an area of learning that held so much promise for the child. With luck, future teachers will be able to rekindle it. In such cases, the parents have an important role in fulfilling the child's need for curiosity and maintaining the child's interest in school learning.

It is clear that for children whose curiosity, for some reason or another, has not been encouraged at home, the school has a vital role to play in fulfilling this important motivational need. No significant learning can take place without it.

Clear and interesting tasks which incorporate motivational questions which give the child opportunities to understand and discover why things happen and how things happen can be appropriate for every age group and each curriculum area.

(ii) Awareness and respect for individual interests

In order to enhance intrinsic motivation, the learning situation should provide opportunities to follow individual interests. Children should be encouraged to invest efforts in areas that they are interested in and to experience enjoyment from their efforts. This learning will be motivated by an interest in the task itself and not just for extrinsic reasons such as rewards or normative class evaluation. The joy experienced by the child from these accomplishments can serve to motivate her to invest efforts in other curriculum areas. Children who have not formerly acquired good learning habits can benefit from this approach.

(iii) Mastery and competency learning

All children need to acquire mastery and competency in new skills in order to make progress in school and attain higher achievement levels. Moreover, mastery and competency learning fulfils additional important motivational roles, as:

(1)   Overcoming fear of failure
(2)   Gaining realization that self-effort can bring success.

(iv) Overcoming fear of failure

As a result of inadequate fulfilment of motivational needs during early childhood, some children, as dicussed previously, fear failure and do all they can to avoid it. Any situation in which their work is evaluated presents a real threat. Some, as a result, suffer from tension and anxiety before taking any tests. This test anxiety prevents them from showing what they know (Sarason, 1980).

(v) Gaining realization that self effort can bring success

When socialization patterns at home deprive the child of the opportunities to internalize the relationship between effort and result and thus gain understanding of the process of cause and effect, they cannot be expected to be motivated at school to invest efforts in their learning, particularly when tasks and assignments seem too difficult to them. These children need more assurance from their teacher than do other children in the class, that they can cope with their work. This assurance can be provided through consistent information given by the teacher to each child on his progress in mastering skills, and confirmation of his competence which he acquired by means of his success experiences in mastering new learning. This knowledge should enhance the child's confidence in his ability to improve and help him understand that his successes can be attributed to his own learning and not to luck (Weiner, 1974). When the child realizes that his efforts are the cause for his improvement (Decharmes, 1972) he will probably be motivated to increase efforts in other curriculum areas. These factors play an important role in the process of reversing underachievement behaviour.

(vi) Challenge, stimulus and unconventional methods of learning

Since children differ in their abilities, interests and styles of learning, they will also differ in the learning experiences which are motivationally appropriate for them. When the work is undemanding, when success is so easy that there is no challenge, then there is no joy in accomplishment. This process cannot lead to the child's motivation for further learning. All children need a stimulating learning environment and experiences in order to arouse their interest in any learning assignment. Children, like adults, respond well to diversity of experiences. Unconventional ideas and teaching methods can provide challenge and stimulus to children of all ability levels. While Chapter 7 will provide teachers with specific curriculum and teaching methods appropriate for reversing underachieving, it is important at this stage to mention that some children adopt underachieving behaviour simply because they are bored in school. Boredom and frustration can also be the result of inflexible methods and rigid structure which does not allow for the development of unconventional ideas and approaches in the curriculum. For children who are creative and whose style of learning and thinking is divergent, it is very frustrating to maintain interest in the various learning activities when the teaching methods used require only convergent thinking (Hudson, 1966). Prolonged frustration and boredom may drive such children to 'opt out' of the learning situation in school and 'choose' to become underachievers. These children may show their frustration in passive resistance to learning, they do hardly any work and spend most of their time in school secretly reading. This behaviour not only misleads the teacher into underestimating their abilities, but also prevents these children from acquiring sound learning habits without which further intellectual development cannot take place. However, some creative children select a more active behaviour pattern by becoming aggressive and disruptive in class. These children soon attract the teacher's attention and as a result of this they are labelled, wrongly, as emotionally disturbed (Kellmer-Pringle, 1970; Whitmore, 1980), a factor which reinforces their underachievement. This kind of underachievement can be avoided when teachers understand the complex process of divergent thinking and select appropriate teaching methods accordingly, which will cater for the individual differences in learning and thinking style of their pupils. These aspects will be further developed and methodologically presented in Chapter 8.

(vii) Teacher support and classroom climate

Finally, it has been shown above that children who, for various reasons, become underachievers need continuous help, support and encouragement that are essential for bringing about change and improvement in their school situation. When teachers recognize the individual needs of their own pupils they can adopt a positive attitude towards their underachieving pupils and provide the help and support needed for those children who, for the reasons discussed above, were 'programmed' into doing work well below their true level of ability, and prevent the underachiever's behaviour from becoming a lifelong pattern (Fine, 1967).

In conclusion, my experience has shown that supportive teachers can create the emotionally secure classroom climate needed to provide children with the efforts needed for maintaining good scholastic progress. In addition, appropriate learning experiences which provide work that is new, interesting and realistically demanding with ample personal feedback can contribute towards a fuller realization of the potential of their pupils (Newsom, 1963). It seems that educators can readily agree with Aristotle's principle, that human beings desire to do things enjoyed simply for their own sake. Enjoyment increases the more it is experienced. These enjoyment activities are many, varying in the manner and way in which they are done and in the persistence with which they are returned to at a later time. Indeed, we do them without the incentive of evident reward and allowing ourselves to engage in them can in itself act as a reward for other things (Rawls, 1971, pp. 431–2). This principle when applied in the classroom can become an important factor in combating underachievement in school.

CHAPTER 3

Intervention Treatment of Academic Underachievement

This chapter will discuss the different approaches used for intervention treatment of underachievement. An analysis of the efficacy of the different methods for alleviating the school problems of underachievement indicates that intervention is most likely to succeed when it commences at the primary school, before underachievement becomes too firmly established to be reversed, and is conducted on an individual basis by the class teacher.

The previous chapters discussed the problematic nature of underachievement, the different factors contributing to its onset and the characteristics associated with underachieving children. The aim of this chapter is to consider the different methods utilized for the treatment of underachievement in terms of their practical contribution towards helping underachievers to overcome the problems which prevent them from improving their school performance.

While most programmes were conducted with gifted adolescents, their educational implications are appropriate for underachievers of all ability levels. Moreover, despite the failure of some programmes to reverse underachieving patterns of behaviour, they nevertheless yield important applications for teachers which will be presented at the end of this chapter.

Two major intervention strategies are employed:

(1) Counselling
(2) School modifications in curriculum and teaching methods

COUNSELLING

The counselling of underachieving pupils is usually conducted by professional counsellors either outside or in the classroom, utilizing one of the following methods.

1. GROUP COUNSELLING

This method aims to create group processes which will provide both an insight into the problem of underachievers in the group and the motivation to work towards overcoming problems and improving school performance. However, experience has shown that counselling sessions brought out into the open deeply rooted individual problems which the children were not able to resolve in the group situation. In addition, the sessions concentrated mostly on the emotional life of underachievers, demanding their full mental energies and attention in order to gain some understanding of their feelings and their relationships with parents and siblings. Although these sessions sometimes resulted in an improvement in relations within the family or the classroom, the process prevented underachievers from devoting time and effort to improving their scholastic behaviour (Baymur and Patterson, 1965; Ohlsen and Proff, 1960). However, it is important to note that when the group treatment concentrated on specific goals set by the group, some improvement in academic achievements did occur. For example, one method utilized group processes in order to encourage the group members to assume responsibility for their behaviour and school work. Each member had to sign a written commitment to attend the counselling sessions and to improve school work. Members failing to fulfil their commitments were accountable to the group. While such methods can be effective for a short duration for secondary school pupils (McHolland, 1971), younger children cannot be expected to assume sole responsibility for setting goals and fulfilling them. Primary school children need the teacher's concrete help in setting goals and her approval and involvement in their progress (Winborn and Schmidt, 1962; Whitmore, 1980; Butler-Por, 1982).

2. FAMILY GROUP COUNSELLING

Since underachievement is often associated with poor home and peer relationships (see previous chapter) counselling is sometimes conducted in mixed pupil and parent groups. Though this method can result in improved peer acceptance (Perkins and Wicas, 1963) and easier communication with parents and adults, it is not effective for producing changes in school achievements. It seems that the involvement of the classroom teacher is most important in the counselling process (Davis and Rimm, 1985).

3. INDIVIDUAL COUNSELLING

The previous chapter has indicated that both the personality and the school problems of each underachiever are the result of and response to socialization patterns and the school situation. For these reasons underachievers not only differ in their problems, but also vary in their behaviour patterns and coping abilities, and their response to treatment. In view of these characteristics it is believed that individual counselling should be more effective since counselling sessions can concentrate on the child's specific problems and their causes. However, since the underachiever often fails to see the connection between his feelings of frustration, his behaviour problems and his school performance, individual counselling must provide him with concrete behavioural and attitudinal strategies aimed at attaining a change in the child's school performance (Zilli, 1971; Whitmore, 1980; Gallagher, 1985). As teachers have often observed, underachievers have difficulties in perseverance. It is therefore suggested that individual counselling should concentrate on restricted objectives which the child can fulfil. The classroom teacher can fulfil the vital role of extending the counsellor's work by reinforcing the child's accomplishments and encouraging further efforts.

4. TEACHERS AS COUNSELLORS

An alternative method of counselling utilizes teachers as counsellors. This strategy can be effective when teachers receive in-service training prior to initiation of the counselling programme. When teachers are familiar with the causes of underachievers generally and with the specific problems of their underachieving pupils, counselling can check underachievement. This method, utilizing subject specialists as councellors, can be effective in secondary schools (Collins, 1961).

However, while subject-matter teacher-counsellors can help underachievers to improve in specific scholastic areas, on the whole, the effectiveness of counselling in modifying the behaviour of underachievers is not encouraging (Gallagher, 1985). However, the following educational principles and strategies derived from the counselling methods, as described above, can be adapted usefully by teachers wishing to initiate intervention programmes with underachieving children in their class.

(a) Providing individualized intervention

Since underachievement is manifested differently in each underachiever, effective intervention should be conducted on an individual basis. Individualized intervention enables both the child and the teacher to learn to trust each other, to recognize the problems and difficulties that need overcoming and select strategies for improvement.

(b) Providing concrete help

Underachievers often lack the experience and drive needed to assume responsibility for their behaviour and learning. An intervention programme can only be productive when it provides the underachiever with the necessary concrete help needed to take appropriate action in order to bring about actual change in behaviour.

(c) Selecting restricted objectives

Underachievers need success experiences. These can be provided when intervention goals are restricted, concentrating on one or two particular problems at a time.

(d) Recruiting the underachiever's active participation in change process

Change in the underachiever's school behaviour can be obtained when he becomes involved in his progress. Active participation of the underachiever in selecting objectives and strategies for fulfilling them enhances the child's involvement in his work and motivates him to invest further effort in learning and scholastic endeavours.

MODIFICATIONS IN CLASSROOM ORGANIZATION, THE CURRICULUM AND TEACHING METHODS

The limited success which has been achieved by counselling methods in improving the scholastic performance of underachievers suggests that intervention treatment should relate directly to the learning situation. Educational intervention has mainly involved curriculum changes and modifications of the learning situation.

1. EDUCATIONAL INTERVENTION AT THE SECONDARY SCHOOL LEVEL

One of the most comprehensive attempts to treat underachievement by changing the classroom structure and modifying the curriculum of underachievers was investigated by Raph, Goldberg and Passow (1966). This programme was conducted over a period of five years as part of the Talented Youth Project, and consisted of three educational methods, initiated in a sequence with underachieving adolescents.

(a) Homogeneous grouping tutored by a specially selected teacher

The first intervention treatment was based on underachievers sharing their educational environment with one specially selected teacher for some of their curriculum and education activities. All identified tenth-grade underachievers in an all-male school were retained in a homogeneous group for one year.

This approach assumed that a special teacher could serve as an adult model for identification and could also provide support and help which would have a positive influence on the underachievers' school attitudes and academic performance. Care was taken to select a teacher who was interested in the problem, and who possessed the combination of a warm and flexible personality with the ability to maintain high scholastic standards. The group had a daily session of the first two hours with their special teacher. The first period was devoted to educational aspects, the second one was utilized for teaching social studies. At the beginning of the year the children were told by their special teacher that they had high ability, but needed to raise their level of achievement. At the end of the year this group showed greater improvement in their school work, social behaviour and attitudes to school than underachievers in the control group, which received no treatment. However, when the supportive provisions and the particular teacher were changed in the following year, the progress of these underachievers was not maintained.

It seems that in view of the individual nature of underachievement, underachievers need the opportunity to establish a relationship with one caring teacher over a long period of time. This aspect is of particular importance when treatment is attempted only at the secondary school level.

(b) Modification in curriculum and teaching methods

This approach was based on the assumption that if underachievers could experience success in a field of learning in which they had previously failed, they would also improve their performance in other school subjects. As many failures were in the field of mathematics, a special programme in geometry was introduced. The programme aimed to provide intellectual stimulus and establish effective learning habits. Great emphasis was given to the completion of assignments, to correct form and content and consistent testing of progress. For many of the pupils, these procedures were very helpful and enjoyable. However, underachievers with serious problems failed to improve their work habits.

While all pupils showed interest in learning other topics that were not an integral part of the curriculum, their general school achievements at the end of the semester did not improve. Unfortunately, it is not possible to evaluate the efficacy of this programme for treating underachievement, since the programme's teacher was changed after the first semester. It is interesting to note, however, that even the 'problem underachievers' showed interest for learning, which manifested itself in learning topics that were not an integral part of the curriculum and could be further pursued by them individually.

While this aspect has important motivational implications for the teaching of different curriculum areas in any classroom situation, with adolescent underachievers the change process is slow and depends very heavily on the continuous and consistent support of the teacher.

(c) The teacher as tutor and counsellor

The third method utilized the teacher in the combined role of special tutor and counsellor. This approach provided underachievers with special instruction in needed learning skills as well as individual counselling. The two groups of underachievers remained intact for two years with the exceptions of those whose achievements were very high after the first year. An interesting aspect of this programme was the possibility of comparing the efforts of two teachers of very different personality characteristics. One teacher was outgoing, warm and very supportive and succeeded in forming close relationships with individual pupils. The second teacher was very inconsistent in his approach to his pupils and displayed a lack of interest in them. It is surprising that despite the sharp differences in the attitudes of the two teachers to their pupils, the performance of the two groups did not differ from that of the control group.

In evaluating these three methods of treatment it was concluded that:

efforts initiated at the senior high school level show little promise of success. For many of the students underachievement seems to have become a deeply rooted way of life, unamenable to change through school efforts. The three year high school may not provide enough time for the underachiever to build the helping relationship with an accepting and respecting adult and to free himself sufficiently from his dependence on the teacher to pursue his goals independently. Early identification of the potential underachiever in terms of cognitive as well as sociopersonal factors, might enable schools to engage in preventive rather than curative programmes (Raph, Goldberg and Passow, 1966, p. 179).

The three programmes of intervention, discussed above, highlight both the need for and role of teacher—pupil commitment in producing the necessary changes in the school performance of underachievers.

(d) Shared school—teacher—pupil commitment to change

This approach is based on creating a deeper involvement of the whole school in the progress of its underachievers. For this purpose a school-centred programme was designed for average ability underachievers in ten secondary schools in the USA (The Richmond Programme, 1968). Each school was responsible for the introduction and implementation of the intervention programmes for their underachievers. The involvement and commitment of the school staff was achieved through staff discussion and in-service sessions for teachers participating in the programme. The intervention programmes in all schools required a shared commitment of teachers and underachievers to fulfilling common aims and objectives. The evaluation of the project's achievements indicated that:

(1) New programmes can create a climate of change in a school.
(2) Improved instructional provisions for underachievers are useful.
(3) Neighbourhood schools can be motivated to join the experiment.
(4) Commitment of pupils and teachers can be infectious.
(5) Meaningful relationships between pupils and teaching staff can be established through involvement in a common aim.

It is encouraging to note that similar results were obtained by the London University Goldsmiths College curriculum laboratory study. The project, which was initiated to help schools provide the less academic 'Newsom Child' with appropriate educational experiences, demonstrated that the involvement and commitment of both pupils and teachers could result in an improvement in the level of motivation for school work among the pupils. In addition, interest in the project had motivated other schools to embark on similar programmes.

(e) Contract method

A different method of creating shared pupil—teacher commitment to achieving common goals is used in the contract method. An important ingredient of this approach is the active involvement of underachievers in the choice of assignments which they undertake to complete. This method was tried with secondary top-grade pupils who were selected for intervention on the basis of underachievement in English, poor behaviour and poor school attendance. The fulfilment of the contracts involved pupils and teachers in a shared commitment for achieving improvements in the areas selected for treatment. It is interesting to note that the pupils participating in the programme stressed the importance of their own choice of work and assignments and the individual attention received from the teacher (Clark, 1978). As the programme was designed to investigate the possibility of using a contract method on one special subject, it was not possible to evaluate its success in terms of intervention treatment of underachievement in general.

Moreover, since it has been shown above that at the late stage of the upper grades of the secondary school, the process of change has to be much longer, it is suggested that this method of treatment should commence at the primary school level.

INTERVENTION PROGRAMMES FOR PRIMARY SCHOOL UNDERACHIEVERS

The general failure of reversing underachievement at the secondary school level suggests the need for introducing intervention programmes at an earlier stage in the child's education which is more amenable to change. Moreover, as the previous chapter has shown, early childhood socialization practices play an important role in shaping the child's attitudes to learning, working habits, interests and motivation. Since these aspects also tend to affect the child's achievements in subsequent years, it is important to check underachievement behaviour during the child's primary school education.

Intervention at the primary school level utilizes three main approaches:

(1) Modifications in classroom grouping.
(2) Providing remedial teaching.
(3) Changing the educational environment and teaching methods.

1. Modifications in classroom grouping

(a) Homogeneous classes based on ability level

This method entails the placing of underachieving children together with achieving children of similar ability levels. This approach, which was tried with gifted children, assumed that in a homogeneous class underachievers would be motivated to invest more effort in their work in order to gain peer and parents' acceptance. This method can be successful in raising the academic achievements of gifted underachievers since special classes for gifted children usually provide peer stimulation and appropriate teaching methods for children of high ability levels (Karnes, 1963). However, my experience has shown that in order to reverse the whole pattern of underachieving behaviour, it is not sufficient to arrange for homogeneous classroom grouping of underachieving and achieving children. It is also necessary to initiate individual intervention treatment which aims to help the underachiever resolve immediate problems in both social and learning domains. The underachiever often needs to acquire systematic work habits which will enable him to experience success as a result of the efforts he invests in his work. Since most classes consist of children of a wide range of abilities, intervention procedures should be appropriate and practical for introducing into the normal heterogeneous classroom situation.

(b) Grouping children in heterogeneous classes

Different criteria can be applied for grouping underachievers and achievers in a heterogeneous class. However, since underachievement behaviour is often characterized by total lack of interest in the school activities, effective grouping can be conducted on the basis of special interests. Each group can consist of children of all levels of ability who select to work together on a topic that they are interested in. This method can be effective in creating motivation for investing effort in acquiring skills and knowledge in areas in which the child is interested. In addition, the heterogeneous group situation should contribute to raising the status and image of underachievers among other children and help them adopt a more positive approach to learning. However, when this method was tried outside the normal classroom situation, underachievers who participated in an out-of-school programme commented that although they enjoyed the group activity, it did not necessarily enhance their motivation for general school work. They recommended that the learning activities conducted within the interest group should be integrated into normal classroom work (Wellington and Wellington, 1963). This point is of particular relevance, as experience of 'pull out' programmes in special education has met with similar difficulties. Often the 'special teacher' and the children have felt that the work undertaken outside the classroom should be integrated into the normal classroom situation. It seems that the regular classroom environment should aim to provide individual children in need of special help with ample learning experiences based on their interests and strengths which can be conducted both individually and in groups. It is most important not to evaluate the results of these activities by applying competitive norms.

2. REMEDIAL HELP

Probably one of the most apparent areas of underachieving in the early school days is that of reading. Hence it is not surprising that most efforts to overcome underachievement in reading are made during the first years of the child's schooling. It is believed that an improvement in reading would result in a general improvement in school work and thus contribute to raising the child's confidence in his ability to learn and motivate him to invest further efforts in school work. While it is clear that backwardness in reading can well lead to general underachievement, just providing remedial reading cannot hope to reverse underachieving patterns of behaviour. Slow reading is often caused by a variety of psychological factors which need to be considered. Remedial work in reading as a method of reversing underachievement behaviour should be based on an understanding of the connection between difficulties in emotional adjustment and learning problems. As discussed in Chapter 2, poor family climate and inadequate fulfilment of the child's basic needs can produce in the child deeply rooted feelings of hostility which may result in her 'refusal' to acquire the reading skills normal for her age group. However, it has been shown that when remedial help is combined with other activities aimed at rekindling the child's interest in learning, as well as counselling for the parents of the underachiever, this method can be effective (Paschal, 1961; Wellington and Wellington, 1963). Such programmes aimed at the alleviation of difficulties and lack of interest in reading should be conducted during the first grades of the primary school in order to prevent subsequent underachievement in other subjects which rely heavily on the facility in, and motivation for, reading.

3. EDUCATIONAL ENVIRONMENT AND TEACHING METHODS

A more comprehensive approach to the treatment of underachievement entails creating an educational environment and utilizing teaching methods which are based on the special needs of underachieving children. Although the effectiveness of this approach was first demonstrated in a programme designed for young gifted children, the nature of the programmes makes it suitable for intervention for underachievers of all ability levels.

The intervention programme which was conducted in a school in California as part of an extensive programme, aimed at a comprehensive identification of young gifted children. As systematic identification progressed, it became evident that many teachers failed to recognize intellectual ability in their young pupils. Moreover, a fair proportion of gifted children were considered by teachers as emotionally immature and as a result it was advocated that they should be kept in the same grade for an additional year. Upon completion of the identification procedures, it became evident that a considerable proportion of the previous unidentified gifted were in fact underachievers. Subsequently, an intervention programme was designed. Underachievers were placed in a special class which adopted a multiface approach aimed at developing the child emotionally and cognitively (Whitmore, 1980). The educational environment created provided ample opportunities for improving work habits and skills by utilizing an imaginative and enriched curriculum.

The teaching methods emphasized:

(a)   child-centred approach;
(b)   a classroom climate encouraging freedom of expression without the threat of failure or rejection;
(c)   support of peer group;
(d)   good teacher–pupil relationships.

Evaluation was conducted on the basis of:

(1)   Evaluation of achievements.
(2)   Parents' written reports and interviews.

It is encouraging to note that most underachievers improved in the following aspects:

(a)   school attendance;
(b)   work habits;
(c)   social behaviour;
(d)   realistic goal setting and self-evaluation;
(e)   school achievements.

To conclude, it seems that adopting a multidimensional approach to the problems of underachieving children, providing an appropriate educational environment in the classroom and utilizing teaching methods capable of answering children's needs, can contribute towards reversing underachievement in young children of all ability levels.

Finally, in attempting to evaluate the different programmes discussed above, it becomes clear that the role of the teacher as a change agent in the process of treatment is most important. In order to fulfil this role, the teacher needs to understand the multifaced nature of underachievement, requiring the fostering of emotional and social potential in the process of achieving progress in the child's academic achievements (Kellmer-Pringle, 1970; Lawrence, 1973).

Since teachers often encounter difficulties in recognizing both the diversity of potential and the specific needs of underachievers in their classes, the following chapters provide them with practical help for better understanding of the capabilities, needs and behaviour of underachieving children, so that they can initiate appropriate intervention and plan the kind of educational environment and learning experiences capable of breaking the cycle of failure in these children.

CHAPTER 4

Studying Primary School Underachievers of Superior and Average Abilities

This chapter describes and discusses the findings of a study of highly gifted and average ability primary school underachievers, designed both to contribute to present understanding of the characteristics of underachievement and to present and evaluate a new intervention model found to be successful in improving the school situation of underachievers. The outcomes reveal that the intervention programme has been effective in bringing about positive educational and psychological changes in the pupils and their teachers. Furthermore, the analyses of the dynamic processes that evolved during the treatment suggest that a vital role can be played by teachers in breaking the cycle of failure in primary school underachievers of different ability levels.

The aim of this chapter is to discuss briefly the main issues, findings and educational implications of a study of primary school underachievers designed to provide the classroom teacher with practical tools for intervention. The methodological aspects and the full results of the study are presented as appendices A–E.

BACKGROUND TO THE STUDY

The previous chapters revealed that most of the studies of underachievers have focused on the reasons for the loss of talent among gifted pupils. While societal and educational concern for these children is understandable, it is clear to all who have ever worked in education that there are children, at all ability levels, who fail to achieve an academic level commensurate with their own potential and abilities. Although the neglect of average ability underachievers may be the result of difficulties in identification and differentiation from pupils whose poor achievements do indeed derive from poor ability, they may, in addition, be less clearly 'exceptional' not only in ability, but also in the realm of emotional and behavioural disorders (Kellmer-Pringle, 1970; Whitmore, 1980). However, my experience has shown that teachers find it difficult to detect underachievement in children of all ability levels, and need help both in recognizing the problems of these children and in practical methods which would help these children overcome their difficulties (Butler-Por, 1982). These needs guided me in the design of this study which aimed at developing and evaluating a model for the treatment of underachievement which could be utilized by the class teacher within the normal school setting.

TREATMENT RATIONALE

In the light of the individual nature of underachievement, discussed in previous chapters, it was believed that Glasser's theory of Reality Therapy (Glasser, 1965, 1969) could provide a fruitful basis on which to build the treatment model presented in this study. Glasser believes that although it is possible to identify many individual and environmental factors which affect the child's difficulties in school, it is not always possible to change them; however, it is possible to improve the child's school situation. Glasser argues that significant improvement can only be achieved when both teacher and pupil are involved in planning the process of change. He suggests that in order to break the child's cycle of failure the teacher must change the scholastic behaviour of the child through a process involving three basic principles:

(1)   Acceptance of child.
(2)   Recognition of the need for changing the child's school situation
(3)   Undertaking personal responsibility for bringing about the desired change.

Glasser believes that the evolving personal relationship between teacher and pupil may set the stage for change in the image of the child as a pupil and thus in attitudes towards and performance in school. Thus the major aim of my study was to construct a structured intervention model, which is based on Glasser's theory and the psychological and educational needs of the individual underachiever which would provide teachers with clear methodology, easily applied within the normal school situation.

The intervention was based on the following steps. First, providing the teacher with a diagnostic profile of each underachieving pupil in order to facilitate acceptance of the child and guide her in enabling the child to recognize the need for change. Second a preliminary meeting between teacher and pupil in which the need for change was recognized and joint responsibility for effecting change was accepted. During this meeting these intentions were operationalized in the form of a contract by which the pupil set tasks for the coming week and chose those rewards which served as reinforcers. Tasks and rewards focused on one or more of the following domains:

(a)   learning—preparation of homework, projects, talks on subjects of special interest;
(b)   social—organizing a social event, making a contribution to the class with a friend; and
(c)   behavioural—disturbing less in class, trying to stop interfering with other children.

Third, subsequent meetings were devoted both to discussion, evaluation and reinforcement of assignments accepted in the previous week and to setting new tasks and rewards for the coming week. Fourth, a final meeting in which teacher and pupil evaluated the success of their joint efforts and agreed that progress could be maintained without structured meetings. The pupil accepted responsibility for maintaining the change process while the teacher accepted responsibility for following and encouraging progress within the class.

In parallel, similar goals were set for weekly group sessions led by me in which all teachers participated. In general, these sessions provided a setting in which each teacher's individual work with pupils could receive the support and help of both the group and myself.

RESEARCH QUESTIONS

The study investigates three main issues:

(1) The characteristics of underachievers of average and superior abilities and how they were affected by the intervention programme.
(2) The relationship between the treatment variables of success on tasks, treatment areas and selection of rewards and the success of the treatment.
(3) The relationship between the expectations of the teachers from their underachievers, from the treatment and the success of the programme.

SUBJECTS

The research population consisted of 72 underachieving children aged 9–12, of superior and average intellectual ability and 12 class teachers in whose classes the underachievers selected for participation in the experiment studied.

THE CHILDREN

The children in five of the six groups were selected from schools located on Mount Carmel in Haifa, a predominantly middle-class neighbourhood which is fairly homogeneous in terms of socio-economic status. The children of the sixth group—the control group of gifted children in special classes—attended a primary school serving an area of similar socio-economic status in Tel Aviv. This choice was necessitated by the fact that only one special class for the gifted in each age group exists in Haifa, so no control group for the underachieving gifted in special classes was available except in Tel Aviv.

For the purposes of this study the underachiever was defined in terms of the discrepancy between actual and predicted performance, a method used in many previous studies (Shaw, 1961, and others). Specifically, the highly gifted subjects qualified for inclusion in the study on the basis of the following criteria.

(a) Intellectual ability:

    (1) They were placed in the top 2 per cent of the child population in the specific research area, on the basis of a battery of aptitude tests and of

I.Q. scores, measured by the Milta standardized test generally used by the Israeli educational authorities. The data became available after the initiation of special classes for highly gifted children in Haifa.

(2)   The gifted in special classes were placed in the top quartile of their own class on I.Q. scores.

(b)   School achievement:

(1)   Their scores on standardized achievement tests (Levy and Chen, 1971) placed them below the class mean, in three subjects: arithmetic, geography and bible studies, as the curriculum in these subjects is common to all primary schools in Israel.

(2)   Their average school grades during the preceding two years placed them below the class mean.

Average-ability subjects were selected on the following criteria:

(a)   Intellectual ability:

I.Q. scores: 102−110, which constitute the average ability range in the specific research area.

(b)   School achievement:

(1)   Their scores on the standardized achievement tests placed them in the bottom quartile of their class.

(2)   Their average school grades during the prior two years placed them in the bottom quartile of their class.

Six research groups, each consisting of 12 underachievers, were then formed according to the above criteria. These comprised three experimental groups, each with a corresponding control group.

Experimental groups

(1)   Group 1—Gifted in special classes (GSC) 12 highly gifted underachieving children attending special classes for the highly gifted in regular schools.

(2)   Group 2—Gifted in regular classes (GRC) 12 highly gifted academically underachieving children attending heterogeneous classes in regular schools.

(3)   Group 3—Average ability group (AAG) 12 academic underachievers of average ability attending heterogeneous classes in regular schools.

Groups 4, 5 and 6 comprised the control groups, equivalent as regards subjects to Groups 1, 2 and 3 respectively.

(2) THE TEACHERS

Twelve teachers participated in the study, three class teachers teaching in the special classes for the highly gifted in which the children assigned to experimental Group 1 studied, and nine class teachers teaching in the heterogeneous classes in regular schools from which the children assigned to experimental Groups 2 and 3 were identified.

STUDY STRATEGIES AND PROCEDURE

Figure 4.1 describes schematically the experimental variables and measures of this study. (The measures are described in Appendices A and B).

1. EDUCATIONAL VARIABLES

Data for all educational variables were gathered at two points in the school year—once before intervention at the end of the first school term and once after intervention at the end of the school year. All data save that pertaining to pupils' attitudes were derived from pupils' report cards (see Appendix A).

2. PSYCHOLOGICAL VARIABLES

Subjects were tested for all psychological variables twice during the school year—once before intervention at the end of the first school term and once after intervention at the end of the school year. These measures are described in Appendix B.

3. TREATMENT-RELATED VARIABLES

Data for all treatment-related variables were gathered after the termination of the intervention, before the end of the school year. All data were derived from the contracts constructed during the treatment session. The terms of the contracts were agreed upon by each individual subject and his treatment teacher at every weekly intervention session during a period of twelve weeks. Each weekly contract consisted of the following aspects:

(1) Recording of the successes achieved at tasks selected for completion by the subjects at the previous session.
(2) Recording of tasks selected for completion during the following week.
(3) Recording of rewards asked for by the subject.

At the termination of the intervention a content analysis of all contracts was carried out over the following aspects:

(1) Successes on tasks.

47

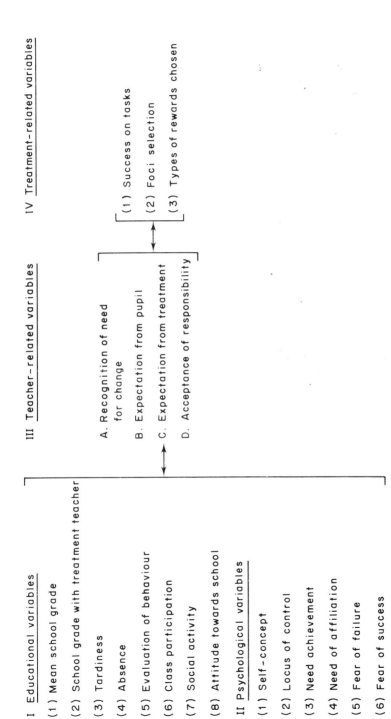

Figure 4.1   Schematic presentation of the variables tested in the study

(2) Foci selected for treatment, out of three possible foci: scholastic, social and behaviour.
(3) Types of rewards chosen (for detailed description, see Appendix C).

4. TEACHER-RELATED VARIABLES

Teacher-related variables were tapped using a questionnaire relating to the following four areas of teacher attitudes:

(1) Recognition of need for change in the underachiever.
(2) Expectations concerning pupil's ability to change.
(3) Expectations from treatment.
(4) Acceptance of personal responsibility for change (see Appendix D).

5. PROCEDURE

After identification of the sample, the study was carried out in three stages, described schematically in Figure 4.2.

Stage 1: Pre-testing of educational and psychological variables

During the first school term, prior to the commencement of the intervention, data on the educational variables chosen from those associated in the literature with under-achievement were collected from the school records of the research population (see Figure 4.1). In addition, tests and questionnaires used to measure the psychological variables selected for investigation were administered to all children in their respective schools.

The data served to ascertain the educational and psychological profiles of the research population and were then utilized to provide the experimental teachers with information on which to base the intervention.

Stage 2: The intervention

The intervention was conducted during the second school term, for the duration of 12 weeks. The model consisted of two separate but related processes:

(i) intervention with underachievers;
(ii) group sessions with teachers.

(i) Intervention with underachievers

The intervention was conducted by twelve class teachers, who held individual weekly sessions with each of their underachievers for the duration of 12 weeks. Each meeting lasted from 30 to 45 minutes. During the first meeting with the child, his school problems were discussed and the general goals for the treatment were formulated.

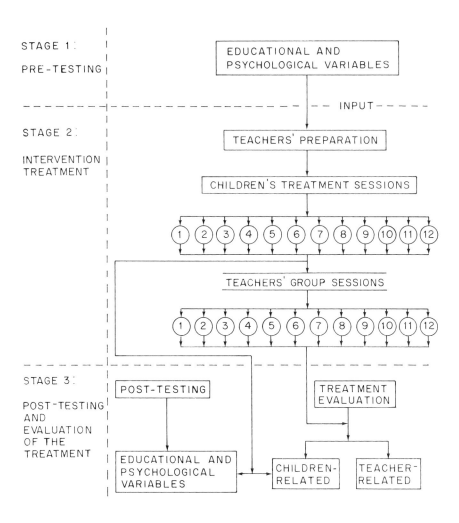

Figure 4.2   Schematic presentation of the research design

Subsequently a contract was signed between the underachiever and the teacher which set out the tasks selected for completion during the coming week. The tasks belonged to three foci: scholastic, social and behaviour. In addition, the rewards that were chosen by the underachiever were recorded. At each session a reward for every selected task could be chosen. A weekly contract was signed for each of the twelve meetings. On each subsequent session, child and teacher together evaluated fulfilment of the contract conditions.

(ii) Group sessions with experimental teachers

In parallel to the twelve intervention sessions held between the underachievers and the teachers, twelve weekly group sessions were conducted. These were led by me and all experimental teachers participated. The general aim formulated for these sessions was to provide a setting in which individual work with the underachievers could receive the support and help of both the group and me.

Prior to the initiation of the intervention, a preparatory session with the teachers was conducted in order to explain the problems of academic underachievement, to introduce the intervention model to the teachers and to provide them with the individual profiles of their underachievers.

In addition, each teacher completed a questionnaire designed to tap the expectations of teachers from the child and the treatment (see Appendix D).

Stage 3: Post-testing of research variables and evaluation of the intervention

(i) Outcomes

The main findings of the study are summarized as follows. The methodological aspects and the complete tabulation of the results are presented as Appendix E.

(1) Generally, prior to the initiation of the intervention treatment the characteristics of underachievers did not differentiate clearly between underachievers of average and superior ability levels.

(2) Certain differences between the psychological correlates among average and high-ability underachievers were found:

    (a) average-ability groups tended to have negative self-concepts, external locus of control, and they scored lower on fear of success than high-ability groups;

    (b) gifted underachievers in special classes expressed more anxiety and fear of failure;

    (c) girl underachievers expressed higher fear of success than did the boys.

(3) The educational status of most pupils improved after treatment. Favourable changes in their psychological profiles were also noted.

(4) Gifted underachievers chose more varied tasks and fewer rewards than did

average ability ones. However, the former tended to choose more rewards as treatment progressed, while the latter chose fewer.

DISCUSSION AND IMPLICATIONS

In general, the outcomes, clearly revealed that the intervention programme utilized in this study had positive effects on the underachievers and their teachers who participated in the programme. Moreover, the treatment which was designed to cater for the individual needs of the underachiever has indeed resulted in an improvement of the scholastic performance and psychological wellbeing of underachievers of both superior and average abilities. In addition, the study yielded important information relating to the characteristics and treatment of underachievement which have educational implications for the learning situation in general and the teaching of underachievers in particular, which merit further discussion.

1. THE CHARACTERISTICS OF UNDERACHIEVERS OF AVERAGE AND SUPERIOR ABILITIES AND THE RELATIONSHIPS BETWEEN THESE CHARACTERISTICS AND THE INTERVENTION

While in general the analysis of the results indicated that the pre-treatment profiles of both educational and psychological characteristics did not differentiate clearly between different ability groups or between pupils studying in different educational settings, some interesting differences emerged which emphasize the important role of the school environment. Thus, while gifted underachievers studying in special classes in Haifa rated more favourably prior to the initiation of the intervention treatment on some educational and personality characteristics, this group also revealed a relatively high incidence of tardiness and absence. These findings suggest that even a favourable environment is failing to meet certain important needs of underachieving pupils.

Similarly, most other groups show a similar pattern of mixed high and low ratings on the different variables. This pattern seems to suggest first that different kinds of educational settings, as special versus regular classes, do not in themselves have clearly different impacts on the adjustment and functioning of underachievers. However, in this context it is important to discuss what seems to be the most striking pattern to emerge from an analysis of the educational variables—the consistently low ratings of the average underachievers in the experimental group. They were rated lowest on all variables except for tardiness and absence—where they were rated next to worst! That this pattern is not necessarily typical of all average underachievers is revealed by the results for the control group, whose ratings were scattered, as were those of other groups. How is one to interpret these results? It seems that the crucial factor may lie in the educational environment from which the experimental group was drawn.

This area is characterized by a high proportion of professional parents whose perceptions and expectations from the school have been shown to be very achievement-oriented, a factor also reflected in the school's ethos (Butler and Butler, 1979). In contrast, some of the pupils in the average control group were drawn from schools in an annexing area of Haifa thought demographically equivalent to the 'experimental' schools, which serve a slightly less professional neighbourhood and apparently are characterized by less clear high aspirations as regards pupil achievement. Thus it seems reasonable to suggest that the more negative picture received for average-ability underachievers in the experimental group reflects their position as weak pupils in a highly achievement-oriented educational environment. These findings emphasize the effects of educational environments and teacher perceptions and expectations on pupils' performance, and support previous findings such as Rosenthal and Jacobson's dramatic study of what they called *Pygmalion in the Classroom* (1968), and more recent findings reported by Rutter *et al.* (1979) who found that teacher expectations correlated significantly with both behavioural and academic outcomes.

An example of the low expectations of teachers with regard to the average-ability underachievers was provided by an experimental teacher during one of the group sessions who stated that: 'Since Yossi anyway could not understand what was going on in the class, I thought that it would not do him any harm to spend some of his time playing in the remedial classroom!'

In addition, it is important to note that one other group is also rated fairly consistently low on all measures—the experimental group of gifted children attending regular classes drawn from the same schools, and sometimes even from the same teachers as the average-ability experimental group. Again, the relatively poor performance of these pupils cannot be attributed to their attendance in regular classes *per se*, since the control group, drawn also from other schools, show a more positive picture.

In conclusion, the resulting clear picture of school and teacher influence on underachievers seems of considerable educational value, since it reinforces still further the rationale for this study—the role of the school environment in both reinforcing and overcoming underachieving patterns of behaviour.

On the whole, the findings as regards the distribution of psychological variables in the various groups were similar to those for educational measures. While certain individual groups revealed patterns which make psychological sense, such as the special classes in Haifa, characterized by a relatively positive self-concept, and internal locus of control. On the other hand, they seem to be in conflict about academic success, with their low need achievement quite possibly reflecting their relatively strong fear of both failure and success. When both such motives are strong it is hardly surprising that a common tactic is to avoid the conflictual field, or in other words to adopt an underachieving pattern (Atkinson, 1958).

There do, however, seem to be certain interesting differences between the psychological correlates of underachievement among pupils of average and high ability. Both average ability groups tend to have negative self-concepts and an external locus of control, and both score lower than the high ability groups on fear of success. This pattern suggests that, unlike the gifted underachiever who may tend, even if functioning below true level, to be aware of her ability, at least, in some areas, the average underachiever may perceive himself as he is perceived by others—as a failing pupil with little to recommend him. This speculation is consistent with the results of a study on Israeli underachievers (Ziv, 1975) which revealed that the self-concept of gifted underachievers was higher than that of average-ability underachievers. The low fear of success is consistent with Horner's conceptualization (1968), by which the conflicts about success reflected in the fear of success score are to be expected only in circumstances of experienced or attainable success. Average ability students who neither succeed nor expect to will thus not experience conflicts about success.

In relation to this variable, it is important to note that girls scored significantly higher than boys in all groups. This is consistent not only with Horner's original findings but also with more recent research on secondary school pupils in Israel (Butler and Nisan, 1975). It is interesting that the motive appeared earlier in the gifted subjects of this sample than in same age samples reported elsewhere in the literature. If so, this may be attributable both to the generally accelerated development of intellectually gifted children and, possibly, to the relevance of conflicts around success for bright children caught in underachieving patterns. It is possible that conflict around realizing high intellectual potential may be stronger for the underachieving girls facing not only internal but also societal ambivalence about achieving (Butler and Nisan, 1975).

Finally, on the whole, while the pre-treatment differences found among the various groups emphasize both the individual nature of underachievement and the interaction between individual dynamics and educational environments, the analysis of the post-treatment group profiles reveal a clear difference between the experimental and control groups. All experimental groups improved significantly in all the educational variables as well as on some of the psychological measures. It is most interesting to note that the two 'problematic' groups of average ability and gifted pupils in regular classes tended to improve more on most measures than did the gifted in special classes. While this may have derived from the fact that the latter groups were originally rated more favourably, it is clear that higher teacher expectations played an important role. Considering the role of perceptions of their school environment, it is not surprising that changes in these perceptions induced by the treatment were very effective in improving the pupil's general functioning.

After intervention the three experimental groups consistently occupy the three most favourable ratings on most measures. This pattern is in marked contrast with that received before intervention when for each group there was considerable scatter in their ratings over the various measures. In contrast, it is noteworthy that while the status of the control groups on most of the various measures tended not to have changed in the six months between testings, a few changes are striking.

The average ability control group, for example, showed negative change on certain measures, and usually on these measures over which the gifted in special classes improved. Thus, while there was no change in their grades or participation, their attitudes toward school became distinctly more unfavourable, lateness and absence increased and there was a slight change for the worse in their behaviour ratings. These changes may reflect increasing frustration in an environment which failed to identify them as underachievers or the increasing impatience of teachers with pupils who fail to improve their poor achievements during the school year. This interpretation is supported by the findings of Whitmore (1980) which suggest that in view of the unfavourable attitudes of teachers to underachievement, lack of intervention may well result in further deterioration.

While the intervention resulted in favourable change over all educational variables, such a degree of change was hardly to be expected with respect to the psychological variable, since several of these are assumed to reflect underlying motives which are resistant to change, at least in the short term. Despite this, the results revealed a similar pattern, if slightly less strong, to that received for the educational variables. Thus while there were no real changes in any group on need affiliation and fear of success, all the experimental groups shared favourable changes in internality of locus of control, in need achievement and in fear of failure, which decreased. It is important to note that on the whole the greatest positive changes were in the two groups apparently most problematic prior to treatment—the average ability and gifted in regular classes. Thus the findings for the psychological variables reinforce the argument developed above—that these groups were most out of tune with their school environments and thus most responsive to an intervention programme designed and carried out within the school itself. As these findings are relevant to the school functioning of underachievers, they need to be discussed in greater depth.

As regards self-concept, both average ability and gifted in regular class experimental groups show marked increases in positive self-concept. This finding is consistent with several research findings which emphasize the centrality of the school experience in shaping the underachiever's self-concept. In their study of underachievers, Raph, Goldberg and Passow concluded that 'school achievement and its accompanying recognition and status were more effective than was measured intelligence in shaping self-appraisal of abilities' (1966, p. 98). Thus it seems that experiences of failure and academic performance below potential probably depressed these underachievers' self-concept, while growing success, competence, and approval during the intervention served to improve it. Since during the school years most of the experiences relevant to this dimension are provided by the school, especially in the case of the average ability pupil, it is hardly surprising that self-concept was so responsive to improvement in the school situation. If it is so clear how the treatment affected self-concept, one may well ask why the third experimental group—the gifted in special classes—showed a decrease rather than an increase in self-concept after intervention. It should be remembered, however, that while change was in the opposite direction to that expected, this group rated highest of all on self-concept both before and after treatment. As discussed above, the literature suggests that the self-concept of gifted underachievers is not always negative (Ziv, 1975) and one may even venture that this study's sample of gifted in special classes may have been unrealistically high. Awareness of their giftedness, together with their having been selected for a special class may have encouraged a generally positive self-concept which failed to take areas of difficulty into account. Thus, one of the effects of the intervention for these pupils may have been to enable them to come to terms with their problems and to view themselves in a more realistic and adaptive way.

The above explanations are reinforced by the pattern received for locus of control, where all experimental groups, including the gifted in special classes, showed significant shifts in the direction of greater internality. These positive effects of intervention in the school on locus of control were also revealed by Bar Tal and Zohar (1977) and by Charlton (1980). Moreover, the treatment itself was designed as a self-evaluative and self-corrective process, two dimensions directly relevant to internality of locus of control.

Similar trends were found for need achievement. Here too, the gifted in special classes, previously high in fear of failure and strikingly low on need achievement, revealed the greatest positive changes in both variables after treatment. It is possible that just because of their high ability, which was recognized prior to intervention, together with the problems behind their underachievement, which were not, the fear of revealing themselves as failures may have been particularly strong. The dual experiences of acceptance of the teacher together with the successful accomplishment of challenges seems to have primarily reduced their fear of failure and as a result reduced the tendency to avoid situations. Similar patterns were found also in the other experimental groups.

In contrast, the fate of one control group—the average-ability underachievers—was different. As with the educational variables, so on the various psychological measures these subjects have deteriorated most. Sad as it is, this pattern served to reinforce the general argument developed above as to close links between educational achievement and psychological well-being, especially among underachievers for whom both fields are problematic.

2. THE RELATIONSHIPS BETWEEN TREATMENT VARIABLES AND TREATMENT SUCCESS

As I have stated above, three treatment variables—success of task completion, choice of foci for treatment and reward selection—seemed relevant to the success of the treatment. As the results generally indicated, more pupils were able successfully to accomplish more tasks during later than in earlier treatment sessions. It is important to ask what in the treatment enabled pupils to succeed in the tasks over a period of time?

Task completion

Examination of success over individual meetings showed that in all groups, progress was not steady throughout the programme. In every group one can find some meetings in which the pupils apparently regressed, succeeding less on tasks than they had done previously.

The decrease of success after the first few meetings may be attributed to the tendency of teachers to change too quickly from continuous to intermittent reinforcement. Indeed the analysis of the group sessions reveals that teachers tended to be very enthusiastic over success in the first sessions, and to assume too quickly that the problem had been solved and that the pupil was already less needy of support and reinforcement in both class and treatment sessions.

It is important to note that these two tendencies were transient, and that towards the end of the treatment, success again increased to a level even beyond the early one. It is evident that the resumption of teacher's support and the factor that the child himself chose the nature and intensity of tasks contributed to the success of the treatment. In addition, each subsequent session focused not only on future tasks, but also on evaluation of past performance enabling the child to receive knowledge about the results of his efforts. This last aspect was found to have positive effects on school performance (Nisan and Butler, 1979).

AREAS SELECTED FOR TREATMENT

The main question examined differential preferences among gifted and average-ability underachievers as regards the number of treatment foci chosen. It was believed that intervention with gifted underachievers was more successful when treatment covered a wide range of problems not limited to the sphere of studies alone. The expectation from the average-ability pupils was different. Since their problem with achievement was not only one of discrepancy between potential and performance but also between their achievements and those of the rest of the class, it was assumed that not only would they tend to focus on educational assignments, but also they would be more successful when their attention was concentrated on that area which most clearly symbolized and contributed to their difficulties in day-to-day living and adjustment. The results clearly confirmed my assumptions that the gifted did indeed choose more foci than the average underachievers, indicating that the ability of the gifted to see relationships and to generalize enables them to comprehend the complexity of their problem. In contrast, the average-ability pupils focused mainly on their educational achievements. Moreover, concentration on this one field yielded improvement relative to their pre-treatment status no less dramatic than that of the gifted children. These findings suggest that, given the opportunity, average-ability underachievers are also capable of perceiving their difficulties and selecting appropriate strategies to overcome them.

However, there are also interesting differences among the gifted in different frameworks. For example, the gifted in special classes chose educational tasks more often than did those in regular classes. This seems to be an outcome both of the natural competition when so many bright children study together, and of the fact that even though the gifted in regular classes were also underachievers relative to their own potential, they were generally quite adequate relative to their non-gifted classmates. In addition, one must not forget the possibility that underachievement among these pupils may have been, at least in part, the result of the pressures towards social desirability. The desire to be similar to and accepted by one's peers has frequently been cited as one cause of poor achievement, especially among the gifted (Coleman, 1961, 1965; Tannenbaum, 1962).

Finally it is interesting that underachievers of average ability chose slightly more social and disciplinary tasks in later as compared with earlier meetings. It is possible that as their competence and confidence in their educational abilities increased, they felt freer to become aware of other problematic areas as well. Thus we might speculate that were the intervention to have continued, these pupils too might have arrived at the more complex understanding of their difficulties.

PATTERNS IN THE SELECTION OF REWARDS

One of the most interesting findings of this study relates to the nature of the 'rewards' requested. Moreover, a close examination of the categories and patterns of the requests for rewards yields important implications both for appreciating the role of intrinsic motivation in children's learning, in general, and for the education of underachievers, in particular.

Categories of requested rewards

Generally, the rewards requested both by the average-ability and by the gifted underachievers seem to reflect their needs at the time.

Requests for knowledge of results

It is interesting to note that underachievers of all ability levels often requested as 'rewards' that their teacher should comment on and evaluate their general school work, as well as performance of treatment tasks. These requests suggest that underachievers need continuous feedback and reinforcement from their teachers. This category seems to reflect intrinsic needs for further knowledge of results of efforts invested (McClinton and Avermaet, 1975) and non-judgemental feedback (Nisan and Butler, 1979).

Requests for 'allocation of resources'

A considerable proportion of the requests for rewards consisted of requests for 'trade-offs' within the same focus area. For example, a pupil agreed to improve reading aloud in English for a requested reward that the teacher undertake to declare a temporary 'cease-fire' on her spelling mistakes in English. Requests of this kind seem to reflect the awareness of the pupil of her own capabilities, and a realization that extra effort in one field will have to be at the expense of less in another—at least in the short run. Thus this category may be labelled as request for legitimization for 'allocation of resources' and does not involve an extrinsic reward in the usual sense.

Requests that success in one area be awarded by attention in another

Some of the requests for rewards were not directly related to the task. For example, one pupil agreed to devote an hour a day to homework for a reward of arranging a nature corner for the class. This category seems to reflect a strategy of 'killing two birds with one stone', as in the example above, a chance to acquire social status in return for educational improvement—both task and reward involve the pupil in investing effort to satisfy intrinsic needs for competence, mastery and recognition (White, 1959).

Requests for self-regulation of reinforcements

Quite a few rewards requested called for self-regulation in one field; for example, undertaking not to whistle in class during lesson time, in order to be awarded the opportunity to devote more time to something that the child really enjoyed—in this case cataloguing the class library. This category involves the child in setting hierarchical reinforcements (Premack, 1959), agreeing to improve performance in a less-liked field in exchange for the opportunity to satisfy needs in a more-liked field. This category seems to be more 'extrinsic' than the previous ones, at least in terms of the distant connection between behaviour and reward.

Requests for unrelated privileges

The last category seems quite extrinsic. The reward requested seems to bear no innate or necessary relationship to the behaviour undertaken. For example, to improve spelling in exchange for being allowed not to wear a uniform for one week. In terms of attribution theory, the situation seems to be one in which behaviour will be attributed to the outcome rather than to any satisfaction derived from the performance itself (Heider, 1965; Kelley, 1967; Bem, 1972). The pupil in the example mentioned above will probably explain to herself that she is going to work on spelling in order to win the desired privilege of one uniformless week.

Patterns in the selection of rewards

An interesting trend was revealed when the frequency of the requests for rewards over the different sessions was analysed (see Appendix E). While gifted underachievers did not make any requests for rewards in the first few treatment sessions, they gradually began making such requests. In contrast, average-ability pupils initially consistently requested rewards, whereas these rewards declined dramatically towards the end of the treatment.

How can these intriguing patterns be explained? It is possible that teacher recognition and understanding of their gifted underachievers' difficulties, together with the praise and approval showered on them in initial treatment meetings provided so many reinforcements of one kind or another that pupils really felt no need for anything further. In addition, intrinsic needs were satisfied by their success on the treatment tasks. However, as revealed by the teachers during the group sessions, the very fact that these pupils were of superior ability and improved dramatically from the outset often served to encourage teacher expectations that were unrealistically high. Thus several teachers fell into the trap of thinking the problem solved after the first few sessions, a change in perception which, by their own report, resulted in a decrease in the attention and praise given to the underachiever. It seems that this generated the need to request the reinforcement that had previously been spontaneously forthcoming. At the same time, as revealed by the protocols of the group meetings, it is surprising how many gifted pupils' requests were for teacher attention to be directed to intrinsic needs—for detailed evaluation of an essay, for comments on homework and so on. Thus it seems that the increased requests fall into two main groups: those seeking to return to a previously high level of social approval and reinforcement and those seeking to improve performance through enhancing intrinsic needs for self-evaluation (Decharmes, 1968).

In contrast, expectations and attitude regarding the average-ability underachiever were initially low and negative, while the pupils' own self-image and confidence were correspondingly poor. Thus, it is hardly surprising that at the beginning they had little basis for obtaining satisfaction from intrinsic sources, especially as their initial critical choices of tasks were not always appropriate and their rate of success was lower than in the other groups. In such constellations, children seek extrinsic rewards and reassurance. This tendency became even more marked in sessions 4−6, possibly as a reflection of their enjoyment of the transformation of teacher figures previously perceived as critical and denying, into people who were understanding and giving. From session 7, one suddenly finds a fairly dramatic decline in such requests, as reported by the teachers themselves. It seems that the increased confidence in their own abilities increased recognition that learning could be satisfying and pleasurable, and increased comfort in their relationship with the teacher enabled these pupils to transfer, on their own initiative, from more extrinsic to more intrinsic rewards.

THE RELATIONSHIPS BETWEEN TEACHER EXPECTATIONS AND THE SUCCESS OF THE TREATMENT

Since the design of the intervention programme was based on teacher−pupil cooperation, it was argued that certain teacher variables would be related to the success of the treatment. This aspect was investigated with regard to four teacher variables: teacher recognition of need for change; teacher acceptance of personal responsibility for effecting change; expectations from pupil; and expectations from treatment. The effect of these variables was studied in relationship to two measures of success−success in tasks within the treatment session and positive changes in average school grades. On the whole, the findings revealed a clear relationship between each variable and success of treatment, underlining the role of teacher factors in pupil outcomes.

The strongest correlations were with teacher expectations from pupil and treatment. This picture is similar to that presented by Rosenthal and Jacobson's findings (1968) as to the dramatic influence of teacher expectations on pupil performances. While it is not always clear how exactly changes at the level of expectations are translated into changes in behaviour, a recent study which found that teacher expectations regarding the achievement of their pupils correlated with actual academic outcomes suggested that 'these expectations will be transmitted to the children who will then show some tendency to conform to their teachers' views of their expected attainments' (Rutter *et al.*, 1978, p. 3).

In more operational terms, it seems that in the present study teacher expectations were transmitted largely through the assignments given to pupils, and through the feedback and reinforcement built into the child's individual treatment programme. In this context, it is important to note the educational advantage of the present programme in which the intervention was carried out by the classroom teacher herself, facilitating the effects of her changing expectations and behaviour to be transmitted to the pupil not only during individual sessions but also during regular class hours.

While the relationship between teacher expectations and pupil outcomes seems predictable and straightforward, certain additional findings indicated that the general relationship between teacher variables and treatment success was in fact quite complex. For example, it is interesting to note that the teachers tended to rate their expectations from treatment and pupil far higher than they rated recognition of need for change and acceptance of personal responsibility for change.

It seems that the intervention programme created a generalized expectancy for a favourable outcome which affected perceptions of both pupil and treatment in similar ways. This argument is further supported by the high intercorrelation between these two measures. The very high correlations between these expectancies and pupil outcomes reinforce the foregoing discussion as to the potent influence of patterns of expectation. A more intriguing question is raised by the *low* correlations between success and teacher recognition of, and acceptance of responsibility for, need to change. The results of the present study indicate that while there is some relation between these factors and success of treatment, expectancies are far more influential.

It seems that the teachers tended to differentiate between pupils for whom they recognized a need for change and those for whom they did not. This aspect was revealed during several group sessions, when some teachers argued that several of the underachievers, especially those of average ability, were in fact 'doing as well as could be expected from them'.

A similar problem is also raised by the demand for initial commitment. In accepting responsibility for effecting changes in the underachiever, the teacher must also confront the possibility that any failure to respond to treatment may be interpreted as her own failure. However, when teachers understand both the characteristics of their pupils and the treatment they can form confident expectations that the treatment offers a solution tailored both to the pupil's needs and to the teacher's abilities.

Analysis of the group sessions, presented in the next section, does indeed reveal that teachers demonstrated increasing willingness to accept personal responsibility for the underachievers with whom they were working, not only for their current progress but also for their future improvement.

THE DYNAMIC PROCESSES OF THE TEACHERS' GROUP

While much attention has been paid to the underachieving pupil, little thought has been given to the teacher of such a pupil. Since teachers, like their pupils, are motivated by needs for competence and mastery, it seemed important to create a situation which would answer these needs by enhancing teachers' understanding of their underachieving pupils as well as providing them with support and guidance in helping their pupils.

It seemed to me that these needs of teachers for greater understanding of the behaviour of underachievers and the possible methods of helping them could be fulfilled within a group situation which would emphasize that underachievement is a widespread and very complex problem, not attributed to the failure of the teacher.

This section will be devoted to an evaluation of the processes and outcomes of twelve group sessions conducted with the teachers involved with the implementation of the treatment model with their underachieving pupils, which will be described in greater detail in Chapter 5.

AIMS AND PROCEDURE

As all the group members shared a common goal—the effective treatment of the underachievers—it was believed that in order to achieve this objective, teachers needed to change their attitudes and behaviour to the underachievers by means of a process involving Glasser's (1965) principles of:

(1)   Acceptance of the underachiever.
(2)   Recognition of the need for changing the underachiever's school situation.
(3)   Undertaking personal responsibility for bringing about the desired changes.

Thus, the specific aims of the group sessions were:

(1)   To create a supportive group climate which would facilitate acceptance of self and others, facilitating teacher acceptance of the underachiever and embarking on the process of change (Rogers, 1969).
(2)   To provide guidance and counselling needed for the treatment of under-achievement.
(3)   To raise teachers' expectations of their underachievers and the treatment through the encouragement of feedback and reinforcement of the group.
(4)   To promote group cooperation in resolving the difficulties encountered by members in the course of their work with their underachievers.

Twelve group sessions were conducted under my guidance. Specific objectives were formulated for each of the meetings which lasted about 3 hours. The meetings were held in an informal atmosphere which encouraged free and open discussion. The proceedings of each session were recorded by an observer. The method of reporting the events and processes that seemed to emerge from each meeting was adopted from Rogers' work (Rogers, 1969).

The evaluation of the group processes was derived from the contents' analyses of the recorded group sessions, a method (Thelen, 1972 and Diedrich and Dye, 1972) by which the achievements of the group were evaluated in terms of the congruence between the formulated aims at the onset of the group experience and what actually happened in the group in terms of perceived and observed changes. The aims and outcomes are presented in Figure 4.3.

While the perceived outcomes were derived from the written and verbal analysis of the group sessions presented by the teacher at the final session, the observed changes in teachers' attitudes and behaviour were obtained from the analyses of the recorded protocols of the group sessions. The group evaluation considered two aspects:

(1)   Evaluation of the group processes.
(2)   Analysis of the efficacy and applicability of the treatment model.

(1) THE EVALUATION OF THE GROUP PROCESSES

The analysis of the group members' evaluation of the processes that emerged in the group indicated that in general all the objectives which were formulated initially were accomplished. Specifically, teachers agreed first, that a supportive group climate was achieved which facilitated acceptance of self and others, a process which resulted in the ability to accept the underachiever. The discussion of this aspect revealed that the climate of acceptance which prevailed in the group resulted in changes in the teachers' initial attitudes to the underachievers. For example, one teacher who had initially expressed strong objections to one of her underachievers, expressing the view that he was unintelligent and that his school achievements merely reflected his capabilities and that she could do nothing for him, reported later on that:

> Doron has clearly demonstrated his ability to change his negative attitude to school, has made progress in all subjects, has selected an imaginative and complex environmental study project, and has proved (to her) that every child could improve if he received encouragement and support.

This finding is supported by Rogers (1970) who indicated that self-acceptance is the beginning of change. Second, members agreed that the guidance which they received within the group enabled them to gain insight into the problems of their underachievers and to bring about the necessary changes in their own behaviour and in that of the underachiever. Third, the feedback and reinforcement provided within the group increased the teachers' expectations from the underachiever and the treatment, and thus provided the motivation both to proceed and to succeed with the treatment. Fourth, the interest and involvement of the group in the teachers' personal progress with the underachievers increased the teachers' involvement with the children, resulting in commitment to the children's progress and acceptance of personal responsibility for the success of the treatment. Fifth, the experience of sharing with the group the difficulties encountered in the treatment as well as the cooperation in obtaining solutions through the modifications in the learning—teaching situation, resulted in the development of openness to change and innovation in the participants' class teaching in general and in their approach to the underachiever in particular. For example, one group member observed that the encouragement she received from the group enabled her to venture out of the

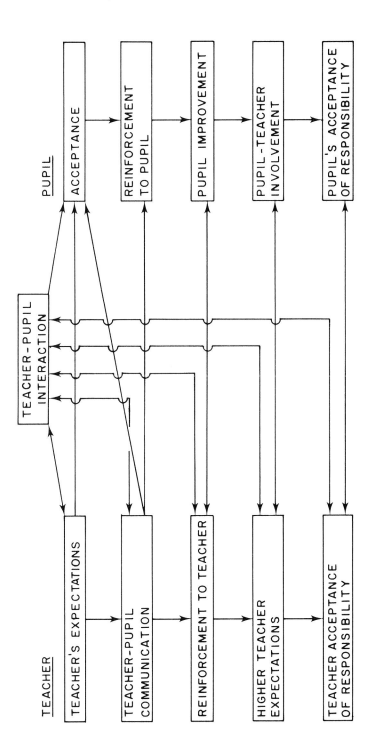

Figure 4.3   Developmental stages of the intervention programme

isolation of the classroom and motivated her to share her doubts and experiences with the group. Thus the group processes played a vital role, not only in fostering greater understanding of the underachiever, but also in doing much to prevent relapse into discouragement and disappointment after an unfruitful session or week with one's pupil. Thus the programme was able to maintain momentum past the initial phase of enthusiasm and the process of change continued until the last meeting.

2. THE ANALYSIS OF THE EFFICACY AND APPLICABILITY OF THE TREATMENT MODEL

While the discussion of the group processes provided an internal criteria of evaluation of the individual perception of the changes in self and others that occurred as a result of the group experience, the participants' analysis of the efficacy and applicability of the treatment model served a dual purpose.

(1)   To provide external criteria of evaluation in terms of the perceived and recorded changes both in the teacher's behaviour towards the underachiever and in the changes that had occurred in the underachiever's behaviour and school performance.

The analysis of the teachers' evaluation did reveal that most teachers agreed that the treatment model could be effectively utilized in helping underachievers achieve the desired changes in their school performance. Indeed, when one considers the positive results of the treatment as they related to the objectives of this study, one may conclude that these findings support the assumptions that guided this study and which are succinctly expressed by Glasser (1969) that the pattern of failure of the child can only be changed if the teacher undergoes a change in his attitude and behaviour to the child.

(2)   To provide explanations from a different point of view—that of the teachers to some of the results that have been obtained in this study.

The group's evaluation of the applicability of the treatment served to explain the findings of the study relating to the process of the treatment. For example, the differences of opinion with respect to the optional duration of the treatment may have affected the results. While some teachers considered the duration of three months too long, others believed that the duration of the treatment was too short. Moreover, several members believed that the treatment should be interrupted for a while in order to sustain the participants' sense of novelty.

These observations shed light on those findings of this study which indicated that most underachievers registered a drop in the accomplishment of tasks at some time or another during the course of treatment. In view of the teachers' evaluation of this aspect of the treatment, it is possible to interpret these results in terms of a temporary drop in motivation of the teachers involved, which might have affected the underachievers' performance.

To conclude, the positive effects achieved by the group may be explained in light of the congruence which was found between the goals that were formulated at the beginning of the group meetings, the identification of individual members with these objectives and the processes and outcomes that have been achieved in the group as presented in Figure 4.3.

Furthermore, the experience provided by the group sessions has important implications for the treatment of the underachiever within the school situation. It has clearly demonstrated the teachers' ability to modify their attitudes and behaviour towards the underachiever and to accept personal responsibility in effecting the desired changes in their underachievers' school situation (see Figure 4.4). Furthermore, the willingness expressed by some group members to continue with the treatment as well as to utilize the experience they had gained in order to introduce modifications into normal class teaching supported the main objective of this study, which was to create an effective treatment model that could be introduced by teachers into the normal classroom situation.

66

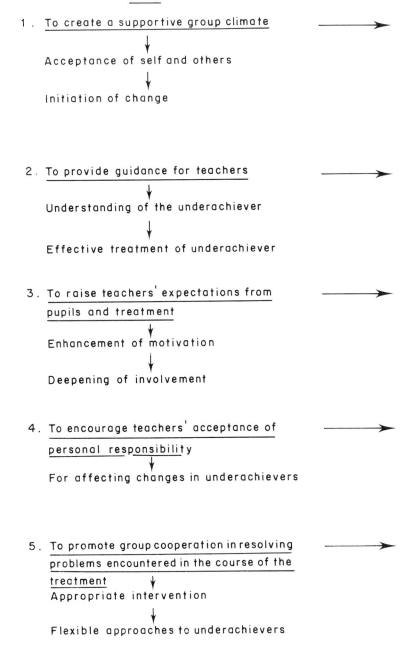

AIMS

1 . To create a supportive group climate   ⟶

       ↓

Acceptance of self and others

       ↓

Initiation of change

2 . To provide guidance for teachers   ⟶

        ↓

Understanding of the underachiever

        ↓

Effective treatment of underachiever

3 . To raise teachers' expectations from   ⟶

pupils and treatment

        ↓

Enhancement of motivation

        ↓

Deepening of involvement

4 . To encourage teachers' acceptance of   ⟶

personal responsibility

        ↓

For affecting changes in underachievers

5 . To promote group cooperation in resolving   ⟶

problems encountered in the course of the

treatment   ↓

Appropriate intervention

        ↓

Flexible approaches to underachievers

Figure 4.4   Evaluation of the group processes

OUTCOMES

1 . <u>Supportive group climate created</u>

↓

Acceptance of self and others

↓

Recognition of need for change

↓

Initiation of changes

2 . <u>Guidance considered effective by teacher</u>

↓

Insight into the problems of underachievers gained

↓

Effective treatment achieved

3 . <u>Rise in teachers' expectations</u>

↓

Rise in motivation

↓

Increased involvement with pupil and treatment

4 . <u>Acceptance of personal responsibility for affecting change in underachievers</u>

↓

Achieved by most participants

↓

Increased reinforcement to pupils

5 . <u>Group cooperation in problem-solving achieved</u>

↓

Appropriate intervention

↓

Openess to innovation in teachers

Part II: Education of the Underachiever

CHAPTER 5

Reversing Underachievement: Teacher—Pupil Cooperation

> This chapter first provides the teacher with effective diagnostic tools for the iden-tification of underachieving children in class. In addition, a structured new intervention programme is introduced. This model, which was utilized in the study of primary school underachievers, discussed in Chapter 4, was found to be effective in changing children's behavioural problems in all the school domains—learning, discipline and social. This chapter discusses aspects involved in the initiation and implementation of the programme within the normal classroom situations.

The preceding chapters indicated that underachievement is a complex, dynamic and individual phenomenon, often resulting from conflicting needs and pressures mitigating against the pupil's ability to function fully academically. Moreover, Chapters 2 and 3 have shown that while much is known about the factors associated with underachievement, and the importance of early detection and treatment in order to avoid a further deterioration in the underachiever's condition, little has been done to provide the teacher with the practical help needed to improve the school situation of underachieving pupils.

This chapter presents teachers with a practical programme which recognizes the dynamic and individual nature of underachievement and is amenable to a flexible individually-centred treatment which can be utilized by the teacher within the normal classroom situation. The programme fulfils the teacher's need for appropriate help so poignantly expressed by a teacher who participated in the study:

> I do my best, as well as I know how, and I am getting sick of people who give me the feel-ing that it is not good enough. I want someone to help me know what I should be doing differently, not just to tell me to understand the child and talk to him between classes!

This intervention programme enables teachers to increase their understanding of the problems and needs of the underachieving pupils in their classes by means of a process of interaction with the individual underachiever. The programme is based on active cooperation between the individual underachiever and the teacher in formulating common goals and selecting appropriate strategies and educational activities designed to help the underachiever overcome his problems and improve his scholastic achievements. Weekly meetings between the teacher and the underachiever, in which the pupil's progress is jointly discussed and evaluated, enable both the underachiever and the teacher to form fairly confident expectations that the treatment offers a solution tailored both to the pupil's needs and to the teacher's abilities. These meetings facilitate greater understanding of the needs of each individual underachiever and enable both teachers and pupils to view scholastic, social and disciplinary problems as symptoms rather than causes of the child's condition.

For example, our experience has shown that underachievers of superior ability often channel their desire for social acceptance into disturbing teachers. As a result of increased understanding of themselves generated by the meetings and their success in class, behavioural problems decrease, as they find more constructed ways of being members of their social group. Similarly, underachievers of average ability responded favourably to the teachers' change in attitudes towards them as a result of increased understanding of their problems generated by the treatment meetings, by increasing the rate of their successes in accomplishing scholastic assignments, and improving their social and class behaviour.

Moreover, the interaction between teacher and pupil enables the maintenance of two very important dimensions of the treatment: encouraging the underachiever to choose the nature, difficulty and intensity of the assignments; and encouraging the teacher to assume greater responsibility for affecting changes in the underachiever's school situation.

Finally, a longer intervention process allows for steady progress and for appropriate and sufficient reinforcement, both in class and during the personal meetings, to counteract the expected periods of setbacks and thus prevent relapse into discouragement and disappointment both for child and teacher, after an unfruitful session or week. Thus the programme can maintain momentum past the initial phase of enthusiasm and the process of change can continue until the end of the school year. Indeed, my experience with underachieving children who participated in this programme has shown that quite often they were able to maintain the progress in their subsequent school career.

The intervention programme which I have developed and evaluated, translated Glasser's theoretical principles into an operational plan of intervention, consisting of a structured treatment plan of clear steps easily applied within the normal school and classroom situation where underachievement presents both a problem and a challenge (see Chapter 4).

INITIATION AND IMPLEMENTATION OF THE INTERVENTION PROGRAMME

The programme consists of the following stages:

(1) Identification of underachievers in class.
(2) Implementing the intervention programme.
(3) Evaluating underachievers' progress.

(4)   Formulating future strategies.

1. IDENTIFICATION OF UNDERACHIEVERS IN CLASS

Since the actual abilities and academic potential of underachieving pupils are not reflected in their normal school work, teachers are often unaware that some of their pupils are capable of functioning at a much higher scholastic level. As early detection of underachieving patterns of behaviour increases the chances of reversing under-achievement, it is important to devote the first few weeks of the school year to identifying the underachieving pupils in class, so that intervention treatment can commence in the second half of the first term.

My experience has shown that the following educational methods should enable the teacher to discover and identify the underachieving pupils in class:

Teacher—pupil personal meetings

During the first school week, the class teacher initiates personal meetings with each individual child in order to gain insight into the child's personality, interests and capabilities. The meetings should be informal and last for 15—20 minutes, while class members are engaged in independent work, thus enabling the teacher to talk to 4—5 children a day. During these meetings the child's feelings about his social activities, school success and failure should be discussed and several meetings with each child should be held during the first six weeks. A record of each meeting should be kept, in which the teacher should note discrepancies between potential, as expressed by the child's comments on his interests, both at school and at home, and his evaluation of the books which he has read, and the teacher's evaluation of the pupil's daily scholastic behaviour as reflected in the quality and mastery of skills, completion of assignments and homework and participation in class.

Introducing diagnostic scholastic activities

Since underachievers are characterized by their reluctance to invest time and effort in their school work, the teacher needs to introduce diagnostic scholastic activities specifically designed to tap the pupil's academic potential. The following sequence should enable the teacher to gain the relevant knowledge facilitating the identification of the underachievers studying in her class. It is important that all the assignments should be brief, and the materials used interesting, productive and worthwhile. The results of each child's work on every assignment should be recorded in the child's individual file. The teacher should take care to note possible discrepancies between the pupil's thinking abilities as expressed by the responses to the requirements of the specific assignment and the child's normal school work, attitudes and class participation. It is suggested that the following sequence should be maintained.

(a) Relevant questions

Pupils are first asked to read silently a short story, a poem, a description of an event or any aspect of the curriculum. Subsequently they are asked to write the *three most important questions* that they would like to ask about what they have just read.

(b) Justifying one's question selection

The following day pupils are given another reading assignment, differing in nature and content from the first assignment. On completing their quiet reading pupils are asked:

(a)   To select and put down in writing the *one most important question* they would like to ask about what they have just read.
(b)   To justify their choice and to explain why they think this is the most important question to ask.

(c) Identifying problems

On the following day the teacher writes on the blackboard the title of one problematic topic within pupils' first- or second-hand experiences. For example: either behaviour in the playground, arriving at school, getting on with my friends, getting on with my parents; or topical and ecological topics such as noise, pollution, hunger regions or current affairs. Children are asked to name and write down *three important problems* relating to the specific topic.

(d) Problem-solving: alternative solutions

The previous assignment is continued on the subsequent day. The children are asked to identify the *most important problem* relating to the specific topic and to offer as many alternative solutions to the problem as they can.

This assignment enables the teacher to recognize creative thinking abilities in underachieving children of different abilities, which are not expressed in their normal school work. This aspect is important in the identification of gifted underachievers since their desire to be similar and to be accepted by their peers has frequently been cited as one cause of poor achievement, especially among the gifted (Coleman, 1961, 1965; Tannenbaum, 1962).

However, though such children may seek to hide signs of their being different, by not studying, by not participating in class, by poor completion of assignments and homework, their intellectual abilities remain and often break out, not always in a way understood by their environment. For example, Torrance (1972) argues that one of the best ways to identify previously unidentified gifted children is to ask their classmates to say who has the most wild and silly ideas.

(e) Critical thinking

Pupils are asked to write a few lines consisting of: (a) positive; (b) negative evaluation of a given experience; (c) the child's alternative suggested method. For example:

(1) the teacher's introduction of a new rule or concept in any subject of the curriculum; (2) a poem read by the teacher; (3) presentation of a plan for a class project, a class outing, and so on.

(f) Critical book reports

Class members are asked to write a short book review of a book they have liked or disliked, giving the reasons for their evaluation.

(g) Personal interests

Children are asked to make a list of their favourite interests and to explain the reasons for their choice of interests.

(h) Personal learning priorities

Pupils are asked to answer the following questions: 'What would I like to learn in school, which is not being taught in school?'

The above sequence of assignments should be followed with a new sequence of similar brief assignments of different content and complexity level. Every new assignment should be evaluated, recorded and compared with the child's normal school work. Possible discrepancies and teachers impressions of possible underachieving symptoms should be noted in the child's personal record file.

To conclude, while the outlined educational experiences provide the teacher with the means to identify underachieving pupils in class, they also serve as appropriate teaching methods for systematic development of thinking skills and abilities in the different subjects of the curriculum.

2. IMPLEMENTING THE INTERVENTION PROGRAMME

Since the dynamics behind underachieving behaviour are individual and tend to differ widely from one pupil to another, successful intervention treatment should be based on the individual's specific needs and problems. The intervention programme which will now be described is designed to help teachers recognize the needs of their underachieving pupils and to create ways of answering those needs within the teacher–pupil relationship and by providing appropriate educational experiences in the classroom. The programme consists of the following stages.

Stage 1. Preliminary meeting between teacher and underachiever

During this meeting the need for changing the pupil's school situation is discussed and recognized. The teacher describes the nature of the intervention treatment and asks the child whether he would like to participate in the programme. After the underachiever's consent, teacher and pupil accept joint responsibility for effecting the required changes. During this meeting the teacher and pupil jointly agree upon the most urgent problems that need to be tackled and select the relevant foci for treatment. These intentions are operationalized in the form of a contract by which the pupil sets her tasks for the coming week and chooses those rewards to be awarded by the teacher which would serve as reinforcers. (The contract is presented as Appendix C. Tasks and rewards focus on one or more of the following domains.

(a) Learning

For example: first, preparation of homework—to concentrate on completing the homework in one subject only and to try to accomplish this task as well as one can; or to concentrate on one specific aspect in the weekly preparation of homework, such as correct spelling, tidy presentation, neat handwriting, and so on. Second, talk on special interest—the underachiever selects for the weekly task or reward to give a talk to the class on her special interest: a pet, a hobby such as stamp collecting, a sports activity, dancing, model building, and so on. Third, preparation of a special project—the underachiever chooses to prepare a project on a particular aspect of the curriculum or on any other topic that he is interested in. Projects can be written and prepared at home, or completed in class, such as arranging a nature or science corner, and so on.

(b) Social

For example: first, making a contribution to the class with a friend—a talk on shared interests, share presentation of a specific curriculum aspect, preparing visual aids for a specific lesson or subject, assembling a small exhibition, and so on. Second, organizing a social event, a concert, a class outing, a sports day, and so on.

(c) Behavioural

For example: first, disturbing less in class, disturbing less in a specific lesson, avoiding disrupting the lessons during one day, for a week, and so on. Second, trying to stop interfering with other children in class or playground. Third, trying to avoid being late to school. Fourth, behavioural rewards may take the form of not being told off in class, or of the class teacher intervening with another teacher on the request of the underachiever to relieve the pressure on the child during lessons, to cancel a specific punishment, and so on.

Stage 2. Weekly teacher—pupil meetings

Subsequent weekly teacher—pupil meetings for the duration of the school year are devoted to joint reviewing of the outcomes of the previous week's contract and to discussing, reinforcing and evaluating the completion of the assignments that were accepted and the rewards that were requested. Each weekly meeting is concluded with setting new tasks and rewards for the coming week and signing the new weekly contract.

3. EVALUATING UNDERACHIEVER'S PROGRESS

(a) Teacher−Pupil evaluation

A final meeting is held towards the end of the school year in which teacher and pupil evaluate the success of their joint efforts and agree that progress could be maintained without structured meetings. The pupil accepts responsibility for maintaining the change process, while the teacher accepts responsibility for following and encouraging progress within the class.

(b) Teacher evaluation

On the basis of each child's records in his personal file the teacher compares the child's position during the first school term with that at the end of the last school term in the following aspects: school achievements in all subjects; participation in class; pupil's attitudes to learning; completion of homework; completion of school assignment, and independent projects; quality of scholastic work; social activity; behaviour; tardiness; absence.

4. FORMULATING FUTURE STRATEGIES

On the basis of the evaluation process consisting of teacher−pupil evaluation and teacher evaluation of the progress achieved by each individual underachiever, the teacher decides on the educational strategies most relevant for maintaining the pupil's future educational development and scholastic progress.

In conclusion, it is important to note that the programme which I have outlined was designed to help teachers recognize the needs of underachieving pupils of both superior and average intellectual ability and to create the ways of answering these needs both within the teacher−pupil relationship and by providing appropriate educational experiences in the classroom. While this chapter describes the operational aspects of the intervention programme, the following ones should provide teachers with further knowledge of its practical application in school.

CHAPTER 6

The Role of the Teacher in Helping Underachievers

This chapter will be concerned with the educational approaches adopted by teachers in helping underachievers of high and average ability overcome their difficulties and improve their school performance. Detailed discussion of the teachers' role as reflected in the reports of their work with underachievers reveals that progress is maintained when children are aware of their teacher's confidence and enthusiasm, participate in determining the nature and pace of their commitments and are able to develop the interests and experiences they have brought with them to school. This chapter should provide teachers and school counsellors both with a deeper insight into the characteristics and needs of underachievers and with practical ideas and methods for effective intervention.

The preceding chapter described and discussed an intervention programme which has been found to be effective in improving the behaviour and school achievements of primary school underachieving children. This chapter will focus on the role of the teacher in helping underachievers overcome the specific difficulties and problems which affect their underachievement and prevent them from attaining the level of achievement of which they are capable.

Since the process of change and remediation is individual, the role which can be played by teachers in reversing underachievement can be best understood by following these processes through teachers' own accounts of their first-hand experiences encountered while conducting the intervention treatment.

The various approaches used for identifying and catering for the needs of each underachiever could be of use to teachers who wish to help the underachievers in their own classes. As the discussions develop, unfolding children's problems and methods of helping them, teachers can begin to recognize some of their own underachievers and try out some of the ideas with those pupils in their classes who seem to be manifesting underachieving patterns of behaviour.

The following discussion is concerned with the entire remediation process. The method of presentation constitutes on-going reports of the teachers on the problems they encountered with their underachievers and the methods they utilized in order to overcome them.

CATERING FOR INDIVIDUAL DIFFERENCES

RECOGNITION OF UNDERACHIEVEMENT AS LAZINESS

It was interesting to note that all teachers without exception reported that they were aware, even before the initiation of the intervention, that the children selected for treatment had a gap between their academic potential and their actual school performance. However, some added that as a result of their problems they did not believe that the children could improve. Moreover, low expectations were particularly voiced with reference to the non-gifted children, as teachers equated high school achievements with high potential. Most of the pupils participating in the intervention were understandably described by their teachers as being lazy since they invested no effort at school and hardly prepared any homework.

The following description by one of the teachers is characteristic of the behaviour of many gifted underachievers:

'M' is highly intelligent. He reads a great deal, has a large vocabulary. However, in class he hardly ever participates. One can definitely say that he is positively lazy. Though he does not intend to disrupt the lessons he is always engaged in other activities such as taking pens apart, rocking on his chair or playing games with his neighbours. He hates written work and if made to do it, does it in a careless manner. The same applies to his exam work. In short a lazy, lazy boy!

The teacher seemed surprised that this pupil was interested and willing to sign the intervention contract. It is important to mention at this early stage of the programme that this child chose to complete the demanding task of preparing a talk for the class on the 'Advantages and disadvantages of urban industry—specifically in Haifa, his town'. Obviously, the problem was of interest to him, since Haifa is notorious for its pollution problems caused by the chemical industries.

RESISTANCE TO ACADEMIC PRESSURE

The question of the desirability of putting pressure on the underachieving child worried teachers. Resistance to academic pressure was described by some teachers as characterizing their underachievers. In most of these cases the teachers indicated that the parents were constantly pressuring their children to attain higher school achievements. However, if one considers the achievement-oriented milieu of the school culture, it seems possible to assume that failure of these children to fulfil their potential in the school situation, a fact which the teachers had been told prior to the initiation of the intervention, made some of the teachers anxious as to their ability to effect change in their pupils. These feelings were expressed in one teacher's report on her average-ability underachieving girl:

'A' is a very average child, though she is unaware of it. She thinks that she is not capable of coping with school work. Her parents are very demanding and exert tremendous pressure on her to invest more effort in school work, but never help her. It seems to me that the child's conflict with her parents cannot be resolved.

However, she offered to help the child by talking to her parents in order to ask them to stop pressurizing their daughter, suggesting that she would help her. She suggested building a closer relationship with the child through supporting her by providing praise in the normal class situation, but believed that no academic pressure should be exercised as 'the girl is very average indeed'. It is important to mention that despite the teacher's low expectations, she reported that she employed the specific method of encouraging the child to choose to prepare a talk on the growth and development of her dog to whom she was very devoted.

Similar doubts were expressed by other teachers. The following teacher's report describes a slightly different approach—helping the underachiever develop his interests in science.

CHILDREN NEED TO DEVELOP THE INTERESTS THEY BRING WITH THEM

The teacher's report:

> 'T' is highly gifted. He attends enrichment courses for the gifted at the Higher School of Technology. At school he does the bare minimum. Though he possesses a wealth of knowledge on all kinds of subjects, he closes up in class. I think that he is unable to face any emotional or social experience. He asked me why we keep pressuring him to do more at school, while he is much happier in pursuing his science interests. His mother keeps pressuring him to try harder at school and he is in constant conflict with her. I promised him not to exert pressure on him at school and help him set up a science corner in class.

In promising 'T' she would alleviate the school pressure, the teacher demonstrated to him that she accepted him and his wishes. She planned to work together with the child on his points of strength and his special interests. In this manner she hoped to avoid the areas of conflict. This approach proved very fruitful.

THE GIFTED UNDERACHIEVER HAS MORE PROBLEMS

One of the most encouraging aspects which emerged from the teachers' reports was their willingness to accept the undesirable behaviour of the underachiever as a problem deserving understanding and acceptance. This was particularly evident in the cases of the gifted children. Several of the reports made an explicit distinction between the average-ability underachiever and the gifted one, who was believed to have more problems. The following teacher's report provides a representative illustration:

> 'B' has high intellectual powers, he demonstrates depth of thought and has a very good memory. However, he simply does nothing in class. He is very careless and negligent in preparation of homework. He has social problems. He is always quarrelling with classmates. He finds it very difficult to accept authority. He never participates during lessons and spends his time playing with all sorts of objects, talking to his neighbours and disturbing them. However, he mainly is a nuisance to himself. So how can I help him? Perhaps I shall ask him to tell me!

This teacher's approach should be productive with gifted children who are usually able to diagnose their problems and find appropriate solutions.

IT IS THE CHILD'S PROBLEM

In examining these observations it seemed evident that though the problems of the children were often understood and even accepted, some teachers tended, at first, to believe that the underachievers should be responsible for alleviating them. For example, one teacher expressed this notion very clearly:

> 'R' is a child of average ability and capable of better school achievements. However, he has no interest in schoolwork or any academic activities. Every method of helping him failed. He underwent counselling and all sorts of other techniques which were used have been to no avail. He is a bully, very strong physically and has become a feared leader. He is a problem to the school, to me, and to his classmates. However, he is mainly a problem to himself. I have often told him that his problems are of his own making and it is up to him to resolve them.

It was interesting to note that though the teacher was expressing low expectation from the child and the treatment, she indicated that she recognized the need for change in the child, demonstrating acceptance of her role in the change process by selecting specific social tasks to work on. This aspect should be encouraging for teachers wishing to initiate intervention.

In endeavouring to evaluate the teacher's role at this early stage of intervention, it seems possible to identify two important factors:

(1) Acceptance of the child's problems.
(2) Recognition of need for change.

In addition, it was most encouraging to note that even at this initial stage teachers were able both to identify and to cater for some of their underachievers' needs. For example, the recognition of the need to begin the work with the child's strengths and interests, to provide ample feedback and positive reinforcement and to fulfil personal social needs, constituted effective starting points for further work.

Teacher—pupil Cooperation in Formulating Intervention Goals and strategies

FORMULATING SPECIFIC TASKS

One of the main problems encountered by most teachers was the difficulty of formulating together with the child those specific tasks which were needed in order to affect changes in the child's present behaviour. One teacher, for example, reported:

> 'M' and I discussed his habit of swinging continually on his chair, which we agreed interfered with his concentration in class as well as disrupting the lesson. Consequently, 'M' selected as his main task to try to swing less on his chair during lesson times. However, in our last meeting, we noted that this task was not accomplished.

Subsequently the teacher suggested that the child should think of methods which would help him to fulfil the task. The method chosen by the boy was that they should determine together a specific time limit during which he would undertake not to swing on his chair.

It seems important to note that though it is usually more fruitful that the suggestion come from the child, some underachievers respond well to offers of concrete help.

SOME UNDERACHIEVERS ARE UNAWARE OF THEIR BEHAVIOUR

The need to help underachievers overcome behavioural problems prior to working on improving their scholastic achievements has been recognized by some teachers. This aspect constitutes a prerequisite condition for effective intervention.

One teacher reports:

> 'N' is always restless and keeps getting out of his chair, running around in the classroom and disturbing other children. In discussing this with him he complained that he cannot help himself, that he is 'up and about before I even realize that I am doing it'.

The teacher added that the tasks selected for the next meeting were to try and minimize the disruptions during lesson time. She remarked that since he was mostly unaware of his disruptions, her suggestion that he choose one period a day only later on proved very helpful to the child, who eventually succeeded in writing a critical evaluation of a theatre production for children, discussed in the newspaper and which she had been to see.

ACCEPTANCE OF THE CHILD AND INVOLVEMENT IN THE CHANGE PROCESS

As the intervention progressed, the tendency to become more involved with the child increased. Some of the teachers began to accept the child as a partner in a joint effort. One teacher, for example, commented:

> One of my underachievers, 'T', is so critical of himself that he is afraid to submit any written work. As he is so inhibited I suggested to him to select for his task, to write about an exciting event that had happened to him. At our next meeting he produced a sheet of paper saying: 'It is only my copy, it will not interest anybody'. His peice of writing described how much he had wanted a cat and the events of the day on which he had received a cat as a present. I suggested to him that he might like to prepare a talk on his cat for the class. After some hesitation he accepted. I am very pleased. It seemed to me that it should help him build a more realistic self-concept as he comes to realize that what interests him can be shared with others.

PROVIDING AMPLE SUCCESS EXPERIENCES

Since a most important component of the intervention programme constituted the strengthening of the underachiever's confidence by providing ample success experiences, it seems important to examine the methods adopted by teachers in order to achieve this aim. Though different approaches were used, most teachers recognized that success experiences can be derived from the weekly contract which consisted of:

(1) Tasks selected for the week.
(2) Rewards requested by the child.
(3) Joint discussion of accomplishments and difficulties encountered.

Since the tasks represented the area requiring corrective intervention, it was natural for teachers to assume an active role in their selection. However, in order to achieve the desired changes in the underachiever's school situation, it is important to involve the child in the selection of tasks. Initially some teachers found it difficult. For example, one teacher reported:

> 'A' has high potential but very low achievements. Although she is most anxious to succeed, she is very careless in the preparation of her homework. Therefore, the task selected was to prepare her history homework thoroughly, and to increase her participation in class. However, I was disappointed with her improvement. I was puzzled that she asked for her reward, to receive a positive remark on her homework book for every correct answer. In contrast, 'T', who is my most gifted underachiever, asked for no reward, though he was successful in fulfilling the task of increasing his homework time to one hour a day, starting with 45 minutes daily. In addition, he undertook to prepare a talk for the class on the way of life of the Druze people in Israel.

This account sheds light on a problem encountered by some teachers who are particularly achievement-oriented in shifting from teacher-directed to child-directed methods. In such cases there is a tendency to select tasks related to normal school activities of homework and class participation. The only task which was actually selected by the child was the one suggested by 'T' of preparing a talk on the Druze people. As will be shown later on in our discussion, this was a good starting point for the teacher to begin to restructure her thinking and behaviour towards a more child-directed orientation involving the underachievers in the process of changing those behaviours that contribute to their present situations, as well as enhancing their confidence that they can engineer their own improvement. The fact that one of her underachievers exercised his choice in selecting a more demanding task suggested to her that he might be able to offer explanations of his disappointing task completion results. Furthermore, the excellent talk that he gave on the Druze people convinced her that she should involve all her underachievers in their task selection, so that they would have a better chance to succeed.

An interesting example of insightful treatment was provided by the statement of another teacher:

> After the experience of the first two sessions with my underachievers, I thought that the tasks selected were too wide and though demanding of the pupils to invest more effort, were not helpful to them as they did not provide them with definite aims and actually left them to get on with it, and deprived them of experiencing success. Thus I decided to discuss with each child his difficulties as he perceived them and asked him to suggest what

he thought would be a helpful strategy in the attempt to overcome his problems. These experiences were quite an eye-opener to me, as I became aware of the children's ability to understand their problems and formulate operational objectives. In addition, it seemed most interesting to note the difference in the ability to perceive the problems between my highly gifted and average-ability pupils.

DIFFERENCES IN ABILITY TO UNDERSTAND ONE'S PROBLEMS

This point was developed further by the same teacher:

> The two gifted children each in a different way described their difficulties in setting down to the business of work. They tend to find all sorts of things which distract them or seem to them more interesting. They both admitted that they prefer reading and discovered that they invariably had no time to complete their work thoroughly and tend just to finish quickly. Similarly, in class they seem to be always interested in any sort of extraneous activity. One of these children, for example, commented that he intended to participate during the last Arabic lesson. But he got carried away and disrupted the lesson as he became very annoyed with the teacher at her punishing one child. 'Most unjustifiable,' he claimed. He added that he would like as a reward, for me to ask the Arabic teacher to cancel the punishment. He continued by telling me how often teachers act unfairly and how it annoys him. He proceeded to tell me that he often gets annoyed with his parents and classmates and suggested that this is one of the problems which often caused him to wander off from the task at hand. He suggested working on it, and selected two specific tasks: (1) to record for one daily lesson the times he got annoyed and distracted; (2) to attempt to reduce these incidences every day. He explained that quite often he just looked for excuses to distract him!

Interestingly enough, this account described one of the characteristics of gifted children, who often become involved in abstract topics and ideas.

> 'In contrast', the teacher continued, 'the less able of my underachievers claimed that their neighbours in class were always talking and disturbing them during lessons. They asked as a reward to be moved near their friends. They both suggested that they could improve their school work by concentrating each week on only one subject. We then discussed together the planning of the contract. Though one of these children is very disruptive in class and I did not think that sitting near his friend was such a good idea, it seemed to me most important to let him know that I believe in him knowing what is best for him'.

The approach of this teacher, expressed in her decision to respect the underachievers' choices of tasks, was most appropriate in terms of the nature of the problem of underachievement which we are trying to alleviate. It should be remembered that one of the basic aims of intervention is the need to rekindle the child's motivation to want to change his present unsatisfactory school situation.

It is important to note that other teachers reported that their underachievers became more responsive and more successful in fulfilling the contract when they were responsible for the selection of tasks. However, some teachers expressed doubts as to the efficacy of the teacher refraining from guiding the selection of tasks, especially with 'the less able underachievers'.

LOWER EXPECTATIONS FROM THE AVERAGE-ABILITY UNDERACHIEVER

It seemed clear that teachers had lower expectations from the less able under-achievers. In addition, they seemed to believe that the less able underachievers could not be trusted to know what is good for them. One teacher, for example, commented:

> Though my two less able underachievers did not manage to fully accomplish the tasks which entailed written work, Bible studies and geography, they tried hard and did as well as can be expected from them. They both selected as a reward to spend extra time in the 'therapy' class, which provides help for problem children utilizing play therapy.

It is evident that the low expectations from less able underachievers have the effect of depressing their self-image. Thus the request for spending time in the therapy room expressed the need to raise her self-concept by helping other children.

Similarly another teacher reported:

> One of my underachievers asked as a reward to help her friend, who is a very poor pupil, to complete her geography assignment. I was very surprised at her request, as this child usually maintains that she has difficulties in completing written assignments.

This kind of reward expressed children's need for reassurance that they are competent and contributes to the feeling of mastery, which is most important in enhancing the self-confidence of underachievers.

TEACHER CONFIDENCE AND ENTHUSIASM INFLUENCES PROGRESS

As teachers became more involved with their underachievers' progress they shared with them their confidence in their ability to improve further and their enthusiasm with the results of their efforts. This aspect is evident in the following report:

> I am delighted with the progress 'C' is making, in all areas. Her social behaviour has improved greatly, she has taken initiative in selecting to prepare a project on domestic pets with a friend and assumed responsibility for organizing children's presentations on the various aspects involved in keeping pets. In addition, she has invested a great deal of effort in improving her handwriting and the quality of her written work. I told her that she could become the best pupil in the class.

It seemed evident from the above reports that the teachers were giving the children a great deal of positive reinforcement. It was also clear that the teachers' involvement in the underachievers' progress served as a powerful incentive for the children to continue with their efforts.

Rewards rejected on cognitive level

Some teachers reported that rewards are rejected by some gifted underachievers on cognitive grounds. The following report is concerned with this aspect. Teacher's report:

I have noticed great improvement in 'Y's concentration in class. Interestingly enough, he decreased his chair rocking and nearly stopped playing with pens, despite the fact that these were activities not selected by him as tasks. Instead, he chose to concentrate on the quality of his written homework in one topic only, in history. He fulfilled his task very well, although he refused to ask for a reward, and remarked that he thought it was a silly idea.

THE HIGHLY GIFTED UNDERACHIEVER IS RELUCTANT TO ASK FOR REWARDS

Several of the teachers were rather uncomfortable with the fact that their gifted underachievers had failed to ask for rewards, though at times they were actually encouraged to do so by the teachers. The following statement by one teacher serves as a good example:

It seems to me that 'Y' has improved significantly in most of his school work, though all the tasks that he had selected were in the area of behaviour. For example, last week he undertook not to whistle in class during lessons. He recorded in his notebook that he managed to fulfil the task for 12 periods and failed to accomplish this task during three lessons. During our meeting I praised him for his efforts. He seemed very pleased and suggested that he would like to select the same task for the following week, suggesting that he could add an additional task of participating in one of the afternoon school activities. When I asked him what reward he would like he answered, 'nothing'. However, he suggested that the class library needed cataloguing and offered to do it.

It is interesting to note that the child, on his own initiative, changed from behavioural tasks to a learning one. This fact may be explained as a result of a realistic evaluation of his problem and a realization that he could control his behavioural distractions. It seems possible that the realization of the progress and the opportunity to discuss the problems with the teachers serve as rewards.

UNDERACHIEVERS IN SPECIAL CLASSES NEED TANGIBLE EVALUATION

A different aspect was raised by the teachers of the special classes for the gifted. They reported that several of their underachievers asked to receive written evaluation of the written work which they had prepared as part of their task commitment. One teacher, for example, reported:

'K' has undertaken to prepare his Bible homework thoroughly and to improve his achievement in this area. He told me that he finds this task quite difficult as he seems to work well only when his interest is aroused. He said that it would help if I could write a detailed evaluation of his written work.

This point is important in view of the fact that one of the objectives of the special class for the gifted was to encourage intrinsic motivation by means of creating ample opportunities for self-initiated learning as well as by abolishing grades. However, as has already been reported by their teachers, it appears that for the underachievers in these classes the fact that these classes adopt a less structured learning situation presents some problems: for example, the description of some of these under-achievers as lacking in self-discipline and unable to engage in learning activities for a prolonged time unless particularly interested in the topic. These problems explain the request for specific and detailed written evaluation which one of the children made. The child understood the problem and could formulate the strategies which he thought suited his needs. In this connection it is important to note that the teacher recognized the need to provide the child with ample feedback and concrete evaluation both in the treatment sessions and within the normal learning situation in class.

GIFTED UNDERACHIEVERS IN REGULAR CLASSES HAVE SOCIAL PROBLEMS

Several teachers described the gifted underachievers in their regular classes as having the most serious social problems. One teacher, for example, was discouraged:

> 'D' would like to be the 'special' friend of some of her classmates. Unfortunately she is rejected, mainly because of her unacceptable behaviour. She is not prepared to change, though she is most displeased with herself, but does not know how to get out of it. She selected as her task to prepare a pet's corner for the class. She too wanted no rewards.

The questions arise: What are the reasons for her social problems? What kind of behaviour is unacceptable to her classmates? The teacher explained that this girl is most untidy, does not take care of her appearance and always seeks peer approval and attention by offering them sweets. It is evident that this girl is very unhappy about her social position. It should be remembered that bright underachievers in regular classes may have a strong need for affiliation which they find difficult to satisfy. When unsatisfied, the situation can seriously affect their ability to function fully in the intellectual domain. Thus, it seems advisable to help these children fulfil these needs. More specifically, for example in the case of 'D', the teacher approached her mother and suggested diplomatically that more care should be given to her personal appearance as this could help her socially in class. These children seem to be at odds with their school environment and need much more individual attention. This teacher decided to prolong the weekly sessions for a time, thus providing more opportunity for indirect rewards. In addition, the teacher introduced a new scheme aimed at providing all the class children with training in social responsibility. Every pupil in class selected a social task which he had to plan and supervise. For example, class outings, parties, sports functions, parents' participation in committees and so on. The underachievers assumed responsibility for organizing group projects, advising the groups in the selection of topics, data collection and presentation in class. These activities provided them with ample opportunities for social interaction.

THE UNDERACHIEVERS OF AVERAGE ABILITY NEED REALISTIC GOALS

A different picture was portrayed for the underachievers of average ability. It was evident from some of the reports of the teachers that though their expectations were much lower for these children, they nevertheless expected them to accomplish the normal school load. An examination of these reports indicated that these children, who were made aware of their ability to attain higher achievements, were anxious to improve and tended to undertake several tasks a week, mostly in the learning domain, which initially they were unable to fulfil. For example, one teacher reported that 'N', who had average ability, did not seem to do much either at school or at home. She was surprised that he had selected for his tasks to prepare all his homework thoroughly and improve his English spelling.

Similar experiences were reported by other teachers. Interesting educational methods were used to help these children in forming more realistic expectations and selecting just one concrete task at a time so as to enable every child to receive positive reinforcement and experience success. For example, each child selected one daily task and received daily comments and evaluation from the teacher. In addition, the child formulated weekly objectives and subsequently monthly aims.

ACHIEVEMENT EQUATED WITH ABILITY

It was evident from the teachers' reports that the concept of the 'individual gap' is difficult to understand. Though most teachers seemed to understand the gifted under-achiever, the position of the average ability underachiever was more problematic. However, the individualized nature of the programme and the child-directed plan of action enabled teachers to gain first-hand experience of individual differences in the manifestation of underachievement. Increased interaction directed their attention to the need to examine in each child the nature of the gap between potential and achievement. These differences enabled the teacher to focus on the specific needs of the child during the meetings with the child as well as in class. It is important to note that as all their underachievers progressed, they became more confident that all their children could do much better.

One teacher's comment on her average-ability underachiever is a good example of this process:

> I felt very disappointed with 'E'. Though she expressed willingness to participate in the treatment and seemed quite enthusiastic at the beginning, she failed each week to accomplish the tasks she had undertaken to complete. However, eventually she decided to select one specific task and to measure the time she spent daily in the completion of this task. Moreover, as a reward she had asked me to read her work every day. She managed to increase the time of work from day to day, and I was very pleased that I could praise her in class for the improvement in the quality of her work. I was surprised and pleased that she suggested organizing weekly class concerts for the whole term. She herself introduced and participated in the first concert.

UNDERACHIEVERS RESPOND TO TEACHER'S CONFIDENCE AND ENTHUSIASM

Several teachers reported that though they were not always sure that children could succeed in accomplishing all the weekly tasks undertaken by them in the planning of the week's contract, they believed that the programme 'works' since they noted that progress was made in areas which were not touched upon.

The following example illustrates the importance of a teacher's confidence and enthusiasm:

> 'D' is a pupil of average ability, whose school achievements have always been very poor indeed. He used to be very apathetic, and did not cooperate in class. During the first weekly treatment sessions he seemed to lack initiative. He managed to infuriate me at times when he selected a task, which he had already failed to accomplish. Moreover, a reward selected, to prepare the nature table, seemed most inappropriate as I knew he could not possibly do it. However, I thought I should let him try. I agreed to his request not to prepare any homework for a week, and I even asked his other teachers to do the same. I was surprised and overjoyed when I saw the interesting and beautiful nature table that he had prepared. I asked him to give a talk about it in the class and to assume responsibility for the nature corner. I was even more surprised when he suggested that he would like to resume his homework preparation. He asked to be allowed to begin with one subject only. It seems to me that his previous behaviour discouraged me and I must have transmitted my feelings to him. I told him that I was convinced that he was capable of accomplishing all the normal school requirements and that I was delighted with his work.

UNDERACHIEVERS NEED TO ASSUME RESPONSIBILITY FOR CHANGING THEIR BEHAVIOUR

An integral component of effective intervention is the active role that must be played by the underachiever in formulating goals, selecting treatment tasks and assuming responsibility for change. It has been observed that the shift from teacher-centred to child-directed behaviour has not always been easy for some teachers. Anxious to achieve good progress, some teachers tended to make value judgments, such as what was important or not important in the child's behaviour. It is important for teachers to understand the needs or motives underlying the judged behaviour. Disruptive behaviour is often an indication of strong affiliative needs which need to be satisfied before the child can effectively check his disruptive behaviour.

As we have already noted, some underachieving children have a strong need for affiliation which they are unable to satisfy owing to poor performance. It is interesting to note that several teachers reported that their underachievers selected a task, to help a new pupil in class. This task served a double purpose: to satisfy the need for affiliation and to receive feedback for the scholastic progress made.

Need to develop intrinsic motivation

The reliance on extrinsic reinforcements as an incentive for learning is inherent in the school tradition. Thus, it is not surprising that teachers sometimes find it difficult to relinquish such practices as awarding grades, for example, in favour of methods capable of enhancing intrinsic motivation. Several teachers, for example, reported that they were very surprised that even some of their average-ability underachievers asked for 'odd' rewards such as detailed evaluation on their written assignments and suggestions for possible improvements. In some cases, teachers report that after a while the same children asked for no rewards. The following teacher's report demonstrates the role of intrinsic motivation in improving the school situation of underachievers:

> 'S' has been working for some time on the assignment she had chosen as a task several weeks ago—to record the development of her baby sister. She asked me to let her continue with this task rather than select new ones. Since she is of average ability, I was rather surprised that she asked me to develop this task as a comprehensive project, expressing her wish to consult me as a reward. I was most surprised at her ability to integrate my suggestion into her plan for this project. She presented her outline and her list of questions that she wanted to find out about her baby sister at one of our recent meetings. I was so delighted with her work that I suggested she give a talk to the class on her findings as soon as she felt ready for it. Last Friday she came to school with large figures she had made on the changes in the eating habits and motor development of the baby, photos and a complete beautifully illustrated book of her daily recordings. She gave an excellent talk and I praised her profusely.

Building on children's experiences

The previous report highlights the important role of intrinsic motivation in changing the work habits of underachievers. Children who, for various reasons, have not discovered the excitement and pleasure that can be derived from learning and discovery cannot be expected to become enthusiastic about normal school work, important as it is. However, when teachers provide the opportunity to build on a child's meaningful experience, as for example reported above, the underachiever can discover that learning can be fun, an experience which can be instrumental in enhancing the motivation for further learning.

In this connection it is important to emphasize that any child's experience which is important to him constitutes a legitimate and relevant starting point for further learning and enquiry. For example, one teacher reported that one of her average-ability underachievers had made hardly any progress. In addition she felt that he was not suited for this particular intervention since he lacked initiative and seemed most uncommunicative. She suggested to him that he drop out of the programme. He was very upset and asked her for another chance, suggesting that he would like, as a task, to write about his collection of matchboxes. Even though she thought it was a 'silly idea' she agreed. She reported that the child started with naming the people who had given him these boxes and where they had obtained them. The child was delighted with her suggestion to prepare a corner in class displaying these boxes and writing up what he had found out about the manufacturing countries.

Slow progress can be discouraging

Young as they are, some primary school children can manifest deeply entrenched underachievement patterns of behaviour, which are sometimes very difficult to change. When intervention is introduced and a child, as in some cases, fails to make the progress expected of him, the teacher understandably can become discouraged. Moreover, when the teacher fails to receive feedback from the child, she may transmit her disappointment to the underachiever. This vicious circle can be broken by adopting entirely new tactics. The following approach illustrated this point:

> Despite all my efforts, 'O' has made hardly any progress. He fails to complete his tasks, hardly participates in class, takes no interest in any of the class activities. During one of our recent meetings I told him that 'I give up' and that he could do what he likes in class. He seemed relieved and spent most of his time reading. After some time, I was rather surprised that he approached me and suggested that two of the other underachievers, who incidentally were making very good progress, should help him select the tasks and even assume responsibility for the contracts. I was rather puzzled but I agreed. Last week my three underachievers came together to the weekly meeting and produced the completed contracts. I was so pleased to see that 'O' had managed to complete the tasks, seemed happy with this new arrangement and asked me for a reward of assuming responsibility for children's book reviews, as he loves reading! I was delighted and decided to let him continue with their joint effort.

It seems important at this stage to highlight the elements that contributed to the success achieved by some of the underachievers in effecting significant changes in their behaviour, so as to help teachers modify their strategies with the less successful underachievers.

BUILDING ON CHILDREN'S STRENGTHS

Underachievers often fear failure. Teachers can help them overcome this fear by building on the child's strengths rather than on the weaknesses. The following report is quite illuminating:

> At the beginning of the programme I had serious doubts as to 'B's ability to bridge the gap that existed between the school achievements of most of the pupils in this class and his, which were much lower. He seemed disturbed and seemed to have some trouble with coordination. Last year I consulted the school psychologist who reassured me that the child was all right. He said that he just lacked self-confidence and should not be pressured. In addition, he seemed to lack motivation to learn which is rather unusual for children in this class who are keen, interested and highly motivated to learn. During the first meeting I discussed his school position with him. I told him that I believed he could do much better and asked him what he thought about the suggested programme. He seemed a little doubtful but said he would give it a try. However, despite the fact that he selected tasks which were mainly connected with school work, the general standard of his work hardly improved. A breakthrough in his situation occurred after a change of tactics on my part. I decided to concentrate on the strengths of the child before attempting to change the weak spots. Thus, at a subsequent meeting with 'B', I suggested that he should write in the contract a task that he would love doing which need not be associated with school work. He seemed pleased and wrote that he would like to give the weekly talk (Fridays are devoted to children's projects, talks, and concerts, etc.), on the art of stamp collecting, and to show his stamp collection and catalogues to the class. He asked whether he could sit near 'D', who is also a keen stamp collector. He then delivered an excellent lecture on the issues involved in professional stamp collection and demonstrated his points by showing his stamps. In addition, he asked his friend to show his stamp collection as well. The class was very interested and applauded at the end of his contribution. It is interesting to mention that as a result of this talk a group of children decided to join him in forming a stamp club in class.

Improving underachievers' self-concept

It is understandable that failing children often have a poor image of their ability to cope with their problems and need the teacher's help in resolving their difficulties. The role played by one teacher is very instructive:

'C' had many problems. It was apparent to both of us that she would have to change her behaviour in various aspects in order to achieve a significant improvement in her school performance. Her difficulties were manifested in behavioural, social and learning domains. Moreover, she was too fat and always looked sloppy and untidy. She is an only child. Her parents are elderly and fairly new to this country. Personally, I was very pleased that 'C' was selected for the treatment as she was really miserable. Helping her presented a challenge! Right from the beginning of the treatment she demonstrated that she understood her difficulties. Nevertheless, she kept blaming her classmates for her failures. It also seemed to me that she was greatly disturbed by her social rejection and spent most of her mental energy on winning social approval. As her methods were disruptive, they proved ineffective. We discussed the situation during her first meeting. Subsequently, she decided to check her scribbling on desks and notebooks, and to prepare some of the homework in a neat fashion. The rewards selected were in the social domain, such as to be moved to sit next to her friend, and to receive monitoring tasks. It is worth mentioning that this so-called friend was not too anxious to sit near 'C', but I persuaded her to agree. In addition to talking to 'C' about her appearance, I approached her mother, who later on bought 'C' a new uniform and a new school satchel. In addition, I devoted some lessons to the discussion of healthy diets to provide additional reinforcement for her need to change her eating habits and reduce weight. At one of our subsequent meetings she suggested that in addition to the task that she had undertaken, to note the number of times she disrupted her neighbours during lesson times, beginning with one lesson daily, she would also keep a diary at home, in which she would record the number of sweets and biscuits she ate during one hour each afternoon. We were both pleased to note some improvement in the fulfilment of these tasks. I would like to mention that I took every possible opportunity to praise her during normal lesson times as well as at our treatment sessions. Surprisingly enough, 'C' suggested fairly early in the treatment to add additional tasks in the learning domain. She undertook to do homework as well as prepare a talk with her friend to be given in class. Though she still kept expressing negative feelings such as blaming her classmates for interfering with her, for disrupting the lessons, etc., it was obvious that she realized that she was not less to blame for most of these incidences. For example, she admitted at one of the sessions that she tore 'F's essay as she refused to let her skip with her during play time. Her behaviour at times was very strange. At one of the sessions, just as I was complimenting her on the improvement recorded in her task fulfilment, she asked for a reward, to be permitted to chew gum! I told her she could as I wanted to show her that I accepted her and respected her wishes.

This last statement indicated the insightful responses of this teacher. It seems possible to assume that 'C' was testing the teacher's attitude to her, selecting a behaviour which is normally unacceptable and prohibited by teachers. Thus 'C' who was a very intelligent child also demonstrated that gifted children are capable of forming subtle relationships with adults (for example, testing the adult for weakness, as in the chewing gum instance, yet willing to accept help in personal matters).

The role of rewards

Several teachers raised the question of the reversal in the pattern of reward selection that had occurred. It appeared that in contrast with previous practices, some of the gifted underachievers had begun to ask for concrete rewards, whereas several of the average ability children had ceased to choose rewards.

The following description illustrates these trends:

> A strange thing happened during the last session with my underachievers: two of my average ability pupils failed to ask for rewards. As in all the previous sessions they had always asked for rewards, I was very surprised and thinking that they had forgotten, reminded them as they signed the contract to write down their rewards. However, they refused. One of them explained that he was so pleased with his progress, and felt much happier in school, and that that was his reward! In contrast 'B', a gifted underachiever, asked as a reward to be excused from working in the school dining room for one week. It seemed a reasonable request as he had broken his hand and should not have been asked as a reward.

A similar tendency was experienced by other teachers. It seemed that an interesting process was evolving; the average-ability underachievers concentrated on the problem which had been most obvious to all concerned, namely, their very poor school performance. Tasks were structured and usually geared to the goal of gaining concrete achievements. These children were happy to select extrinsic rewards, as it was the system that they had been accustomed to. Similarly, teachers, understandably, felt comfortable with this traditional method of reinforcement which characterized the normal school milieu. However, the programme introduced the children to a school situation which was far from normal. They were receiving a great deal of individual attention from the teacher; they were praised for their efforts and progress. They were beginning to appreciate the results of their efforts. Each weekly meeting became a rewarding experience. For these children a very significant change in the school situation had taken place. Their responses indicated that personal achievement served as an impetus for further learning. In contrast, for the gifted underachievers, a different process was evolving. They, too, were experiencing an unusual school situation. Probably for the first time in their school career, they were given opportunities to share their problems, feelings and thoughts with their teachers. The intervention demonstrated that these children were characterized by an ability to perceive the complexity of their problem and to select appropriate strategies in order to resolve their difficulties. They, too, were given a great deal of individual attention and ample positive reinforcement in class and during the sessions. The reports indicated that their teachers were encouraging them to select rewards, as this method of reinforcement was the most obvious one for them to use. Consequently, as they became more confident with their teachers' acceptance of them, they could afford to indulge in asking for concrete rewards, a practice which might have been motivated by a desire to please the teacher or by a wish to adopt normal child-like behaviour which they obviously needed.

SOCIAL PROBLEMS ARE MORE PERSISTENT

The social problems of the underachiever were raised by several teachers. Some teachers expressed the opinion that while the children responded very well to the programme in terms of the progress they had made in the learning dimension, they seemed to make less advances in the social domain. The following description of two underachievers serves as a good example:

> I am concerned about the social problems of one of my underachievers. 'T' has made excellent progress in all subjects. He has managed to accomplish most of the tasks and the quality of his written work has improved considerably. In addition, he has increased his class participation though recently this has not constituted part of the task commitment. However, he appears to be a 'lone wolf', and seems reluctant to take an active part in any of the class social events. It seems to me that he lacks confidence and social skills. I explained to him that it is important for him to take a more active role in the social life of the class. However, so far he has not done anything in this respect. I decided to ask him to undertake some monitoring responsibilities to which he agreed reluctantly.

It is possible that 'T' spent all his mental energy on the accomplishment of scholastic tasks and on efforts to improve his achievements. The concentration on this main objective might have interfered with his ability to invest the efforts needed in order to alter his social pattern of behaviours. It is encouraging to note that the teacher subsequently reported that she had asked the child to take a more active role in the social life of the class and suggested that he should edit the class newspaper and select the editorial staff from children who live near him. Thus the child would combine an intellectual enterprise with some social interaction. This experience, if successful, should motivate him to undertake additional social commitments.

RAISING THE UNDERACHIEVER'S SOCIAL STATUS

The problem of social rejection was reported by a different teacher:

> Social problems seem to be characteristic of most of my underachievers; however, the problem of 'B' is more severe as he is rejected by all his classmates. He is a peculiar child, fat, spoiled and tends to befriend only younger children. Lately, I have noticed that he is always tired in the mornings on arrival at school. During our last session I asked him whether he was feeling well as he looked very tired. He told me that he went to bed late as he had to prepare his school work in the evenings, that he always sleeps in the afternoons as he feels so tired after school. I suggested that he should undertake as a task to rearrange his day in such a manner that he would be less tired in school, and could also have time for other activities as well as homework preparation. In addition, I talked to his mother and asked for her unobtrusive help in arranging a more normal timetable for 'B'. However, I am more concerned with his social rejection. As most boys enjoy playing football and follow the football results keenly, and since 'B' feels more secure and less rejected in the company of younger boys, I thought that it might help to raise his social status in class if he selected a task which would demonstrate his knowledge of the game. He could give a very good commentary and evaluation of the Saturday football results and I suggested that he become the class sports newspaper editor. He seemed quite pleased about it.

These ideas make a contribution towards 'B's acceptance by the children and should help to raise his own self-image. It is important that these activities should be followed up by his own suggestion for further development of his social involvement and contribution in this aspect of school life.

TEACHERS' ROLE IN HELPING THEIR UNDERACHIEVERS ASSUME RESPONSIBILITY FOR IMPROVING THEIR SCHOOL SITUATION

The above reports clearly indicated that teachers perceived that it was their own personal responsibility to adopt appropriate strategies in order to achieve the desired changes in their underachievers. Furthermore, teachers recognized the need for the underachiever to assume responsibility for his own progress. The following teacher's report describes these processes.

> 'D' is of very average ability. Initially he appeared apathetic in class and lacked initiative in the selection of treatment tasks. Later on he became much more interested in the class activities after he had won a great deal of justified praise for his beautifully executed 'reward' job, which consisted of the preparation of the nature table. In addition, at our subsequent sessions, I remarked how thrilled I was with his nature table, and that it was the best one we had ever had. He beamed with delight, suggesting that he would like to be responsible for the nature table and suggested that each week a different pupil would make a contribution to the collection, while he would be responsible for the display and the commentary. He also undertook to take charge of recording this task in the contract. Though the assignment was initially selected as a reward, I suggested that he should plan his progress on the basis of such tasks. In this manner, I believed that he would be able to integrate into the treatment tasks the problems that needed resolving. During the week 'D' was very active in his subsequent task. His nature table suggestion was accepted with enthusiasm by the class. I noted that he had also prepared a nature newspaper which he edited and for which he prepared contributions.

THE ROLE OF TEACHER EXPECTATIONS

Though some teachers expressed the view that not all their expectations of their underachievers were fulfilled, it was nevertheless evident from their reports that generally the level of teachers' expectations had risen considerably. It was interesting to note that several teachers had made a point of admitting that they were actually surprised at some of their underachievers' progress.

However, it should be remembered that teachers can get discouraged at times, as expressed by one teacher: 'One needs to have a lot of patience. Not all teachers nor all children have the patience to persevere.' However, such feelings are understandable and usually pass quickly, when alternative approaches and teaching methods are adopted. In fact, several teachers commented that they often changed their teaching methods and that the programme had stimulated other members of the class and appeared to have generated ideas for new projects.

NEED FOR ALTERNATIVE TEACHING METHODS

The following report illustrates the advantages of selecting alternative strategies:

> 'B' who, though very able, is usually very lazy and restless in class, surprised me by making a real effort to improve after one of our sessions in which he selected as a task to prepare together with his best friend a dictionary of the new concepts we have learned in

Geography. Though his request was irregular as the task involved working with a child who was not involved with the programme, I thought that I should allow it and hoped that this new method would motivate him. 'B' and his friend did an excellent job. I praised him in class and at our meeting for the magnificent job, and emphasized that it would help me explain some of the difficult concepts to those of the children who failed to fully understand them. He was very pleased and suggested several interesting projects as tasks for subsequent meetings.

FLEXIBLE TEACHER BEHAVIOUR

As the programme progressed teachers became more flexible and imaginative in their classroom behaviour. For example, one teacher suggested to her underachievers that they accept responsibility for organizing geography learning centres for the whole class. The children were very pleased. They divided the class into six groups and planned with each group the geography centre that they would prepare as part of the whole geography topic. This idea was accepted with enthusiasm by the class and thus enabled the underachievers to receive feedback and reinforcement not only from the teachers, but also from the other children. When the normal classroom situation is formal, as in this case, it is understandable that teachers who have been accustomed to traditional teacher methods find it more difficult to accept innovative educational ideas. Thus, the change that had been made by this teacher from a teacher-directed to a child-centred learning situation signified an important development in the teacher's educational growth.

UNDERACHIEVERS NEED STIMULATING ACTIVITIES

Since underachievers need to improve their work habits and scholastic achievements, it is natural that they and their teacher should devote much of their effort to this end. However, it is also important to remember that academic progress depends on the development of the whole child. Care must be taken to ensure that scholastic assignments provide underachievers with the stimulus and challenge that they need. In this connection the following report is illuminating:

'M' has complained that the tasks are boring, yet seems unable to suggest alternative ones. He thought that his written work had improved and that he could bring himself to write 'a decent composition'. However, he added that he would prefer to devote his time to arithmetic homework and reading. He remarked that though he believed that he could concentrate in class and participate in lessons, he thought a lot of the lessons were boring. He remarked that he enjoyed the preparation of the lecture he had given in class on the 'Hazards of Air Pollution in Haifa'. I praised him again for his most interesting talk, commenting on his wide knowledge of scientific terms, and asked him whether his parents had helped him with this topic. He answered: 'I never ask my parents for help as the war (Second World War) prevented them from studying!' At this point it became clear to me that part of his school troubles resulted from lack of stimulus at home. The problem remains, what shall be done about his feelings of boredom both with tasks and with school? It seemed to me that I must restructure some of the curriculum activities so as to provide intellectual stimulus through discussion of real problems.

This approach should be very productive for providing appropriate intellectual experience. In addition, it could present a continuing challenge through follow-up projects. It is possible that 'M's reluctance to suggest new and more interesting tasks may reflect his need to receive from the teacher the stimulus, help and response that he cannot obtain from his parents.

The need for stimulating experiences was expressed in other reports. For example, one of the tasks that one child selected consisted of planning and taking charge of group workshops in science for the duration of three months. This assignment provided opportunities for the disciplined, systematic and stimulating scholastic work which is of great importance to underachievers.

SOME UNDERACHIEVERS FEAR SUCCESS

As discussed in Chapter 2, success for various reasons sometimes presents a threat for underachievers. Teachers were puzzled that a few underachieving girls and one of the boys manifested fear of success.

Underachievers fear success for different reasons. In some cases, 'social desirability' may prevent gifted children from excelling in class. Others may fear that success may result in further pressure to succeed. In such cases it is important to discuss these problems with the children in order to formulate a plan of action together. In this connection, it is important to remember that the problem of the gap between the intellectual and emotional development of some gifted underachievers should not be transmitted to the child by the teacher, that high scholastic expectations are related to expectations of a higher level of maturity. In the case of the gifted under-achiever, the gap between the intellectual and emotional development results in the children's need for continuous support and reassurance on behalf of the teacher that they are actually making good progress. However, they also need reassurance that this progress will not result in excessive pressure to succeed. In addition, the social vulnerability of some underachievers should be remembered when teachers plan intervention activities.

CATERING FOR INDIVIDUAL NEEDS

The importance of catering for individual differences was recognized by most teachers. The following two examples demonstrate teacher willingness and ability to answer the different needs of underachievers.

As both of my underachievers had different scholastic and emotional problems, I decided right from the beginning of the programme to work on two aspects simultaneously:

(1)   The emotional development of the children;
(2)   The specific learning problems that were interfering with their general scholastic performance.

My objectives for each child were guided by the characteristics and specific needs of the child. 'D' was a quiet child who had high need of affiliation, but lacked the confidence and the skills to form relationships with other children in the class. In addition, he had no interest in school work and seemed to lack motivation to invest any effort in his scholastic work. Consequently, my work with 'D' focused on both the emotional and the scholastic aspects. During our first meetings 'D' was very uncommunicative and it was very difficult to get through to him. He selected learning tasks that were too easy for him, a fact which demonstrates his lack of confidence and fear of failure. In one of our first meetings, he told me that he did not believe he could change his situation. I decided, too, that I must first succeed in the challenge: to win his confidence. It was not easy. For example, he suggested that he would keep a diary and record in it his daily activities associated with the fulfilment of tasks. However, he refused to show me what he had written, but agreed to take charge of writing the contracts. He also refused to ask for any rewards.

Sometime later I was pleased to note that 'D' had become more communicative with me. The change had occurred as a result of his interest in the fulfilment of a new task that he had selected: to set up a natural history museum in class. The collection consisted of fossils and minerals that he had found on Mount Carmel. During one of our recent sessions he consulted me on the display of the exhibits and expressed his enthusiasm for this task. I suggested that he should ask one of his friends to join him in his outings and help him with collecting and carrying of the exhibits. He replied that he would think about it. I was thrilled when he informed me the following day that 'E' had agreed to join him. At subsequent meetings he reported on the progress he had made with the collection. He became much more talkative and willing to discuss his general school work. He even expressed his confidence that he would be able to plan tasks which should help raise his achievements in all subjects. In our last session I complimented him on the excellent museum that he had prepared with 'E', and asked him whether he would be prepared to give a talk to the class about their findings. He replied that he was not ready yet. But he would try to do it before the end of the term, adding smilingly: 'It could be your reward instead of rewards which you offered to me!'

A different approach was required for this teacher's second underachiever:

'A' is quite different. His main problem was the combination of two characteristics: superior intellectual ability with a very aggressive and restless personality. He has acquired a reputation at school for his emotional tantrums and at times uncontrollable aggressive attacks on children during play time. During our first session, I told him that he was not doing justice to his ability and instead of putting more efforts into his schoolwork, he spends all his energy in fighting! I asked him if he agreed with me. Surprisingly enough, he admitted that I was perfectly right. I then described to him the proposed programme and asked him whether he thought he could benefit from it. He replied that he was quite sure that he could. Though at the time I felt like saying that I wished I was so sure, I nevertheless told him that I was pleased that he thought so, and asked him to select the problems he would first like to work on. To my relief, I discovered that working with him was much easier than working with 'D'. 'A' needed no prompting in talking about his problems and progress. At the initial stage of the treatment, 'A' selected tasks to reduce the incidences of his fighting and to record in a diary each day the number of outbursts and fights he had both in class or at play time. In addition, he selected a project in geography which he prepared magnificently.

Moreover, he offered to give a talk to the class on his project and suggested that each child should select a different topic in geography to study extensively and to prepare a talk for the class. I asked him to suggest it to the class. Needless to say, the children were delighted. 'A' himself gave the first talk which was accompanied by slides and an exhibition. Soon after this occasion he was even selected as a member of the class committee. His progress was indeed incredible. He became much calmer and demonstrated that he could control his behaviour.

He is very imaginative in the selection of tasks, works harder on the normal school assignments and has started a 'help club' in the class. During one of the sessions he told me that as a committee member he would like to start something new that would help all the class children. He suggested that one period a week could be given to the 'help club'. explaining that every child needs help in one subject or in a certain topic, whereas all pupils feel that they could be of help in an area in which they are particularly interested.

He made a catalogue of children requesting help, and a separate list of offers of help, so that during the 'help club' period children could either obtain help or offer help. The club is a great success.

It seems to me that the aggressive behaviour of 'A' might have been caused by frustration of not being able to find an outlet for his tremendous energy and creative ideas. I can see now how painful normal school work must be for such a child.

UNDERACHIEVERS ARE CAPABLE OF CONTRIBUTING TO THEIR PEERS

The 'help club' described above demonstrates that underachieving children could contribute to the normal classroom situation, when encouraged to do so by their teachers.

SUMMARY AND CONCLUSIONS

This chapter focused on teachers' own perceptions of the role they played in helping their underachievers to overcome their difficulties. Moreover, the analyses of teachers' reports of their work with underachieving children clearly indicated that their interaction with these children enabled them to identify the crucial factors that needed to be considered in creating the educational environment most conducive to affecting the desired changes in the underachiever's school situation. The following summary of these aspects should be helpful to all teachers in planning appropriate educational experiences capable of promoting the full development of children.

1. INDIVIDUAL DIFFERENCES: AN IMPORTANT FACTOR

Catering for individual differences in the process of helping underachievers with their problems constitutes an important component in this intervention programme. However, the theoretical understanding of this concept is much easier than its translation to concrete behavioural objectives. As teachers became more involved with their underachievers they were able to recognize that each underachiever, as any other child, had his own personal needs, characteristics and interests.

2. RECOGNITION OF NEED FOR CHANGE: VITAL TO THE UNDERACHIEVER'S CHANGE PROCESS

Teachers' recognition of the need for their underachievers to change the behaviour patterns that were associated with their school difficulties has been evident in most of the initial reports. Further development in this aspect occurred during the later stages of the programme, when they, too, needed to change their behaviour and attitudes towards their underachieving pupils.

3. BELIEF IN AND EXPECTATION FROM PUPILS: AN INTEGRAL INGREDIENT OF THE INTERVENTION'S SUCCESS

The relationship between the teacher's expectations from the underachiever and the rate of his progress has been evident right through the programme. Many teachers reported that as the intervention proceeded, it became apparent to them that their underachievers could improve in any area if they put their mind to it and expressed confidence in the children's ability to produce good work.

4. ACCEPTANCE OF PERSONAL RESPONSIBILITY: MANIFESTATIONS OF SHIFT TOWARDS INTERNAL LOCUS OF CONTROL

The analyses of teachers' reports revealed that the willingness of teacher and underachiever to accept personal responsibility for the changes that must be achieved in order to bring about significant improvements in the child's underachievement, constituted an important factor in the success of the intervention. Moreover, the reports indicated that for some underachievers who had reached the stage of assuming personal responsibility for the planning of their future progress, the process also manifested a shift from external to internal locus of control, highlighting the fact that some children began to attribute the progress that they had achieved to their actions.

5. UNDERACHIEVERS' ACCEPTANCE OF PERSONAL RESPON-SIBILITY ENHANCES INTRINSIC MOTIVATION

A most significant contribution to the success of children in overcoming underachievement was made by steady increase in children's intrinsic motivation. Teachers' reports revealed that as underachievers of all abilities began to accept greater responsibility for planning the strategies needed for improving their school situation, they needed less tangible rewards.

6. FEEDBACK AND POSITIVE REINFORCEMENT: A CONTINUOUS NEED

Practically all the reports revealed that teachers recognized the important role that feedback and positive reinforcement play in the underachiever's change process. Furthermore, teachers indicated that underachievers needed to receive continuous and on-going feedback, positive reinforcement and support even after they had made considerable gains in their achievements in order to help them internalize their newly acquired work habits and confidence in their ability to maintain progress.

Finally, it is possible to conclude that the teachers played a vital role in breaking the cycle of failure in these children. Moreover, in developing sensitivity to the needs of the individual underachiever, teachers demonstrated that they were capable of both identifying and catering to the diverse needs of the underachiever in intellectual, social and personal domains. In addition, teachers demonstrated that they could become important change agents both in helping underachievers overcome their problems and in reducing the incidences of underachievement in schools.

I believe that the approach adopted by the teachers in this intervention programme could be beneficially utilized with all children, thus contributing to the enhancement of their full development and the realization of their abilities. Since these aspects have important educational implications for the learning situation, teaching methods and class practices, they will be discussed in the following chapter.

CHAPTER 7

Reducing Underachievement in Schools: Educational Implications

This chapter will discuss those classroom conditions which can be created to help reduce and prevent underachievement. An analysis of the different needs of underachievers suggests certain specific educational goals and teaching methods which should be of value to teachers concerned with providing optimal educational environments for the underachiever. Detailed discussion of these goals and methods will further reveal that the environment most suited to the underachiever is, in fact, that which enables all pupils to advance according to their own needs and abilities.

The intervention programme described in previous chapters was designed to help teachers recognize the needs of their underachieving pupils and to create ways of answering these needs both within the teacher–pupil relationship and by providing appropriate educational experiences in the classroom. Since it seems that underachievement develops, at least in part, as a result of the failure of the school to recognize and answer pupils' needs, it is important that appropriate educational objectives and practice should cater for these needs. The clearest reflection of pupils' needs, as they themselves perceived them, can be found in the weekly contracts, discussed in detail in Chapter 6.

While these needs, requested as rewards, expressed the frustrated desires of underachieving pupils and their longing to receive appropriate answers to their needs, are they not also a reflection of the needs of all children? It seems to me that the clear picture obtained of motivational, intellectual, creative, social and emotional needs is important to all children and should be answered within the normal classroom situation.

The following objectives, derived from the needs of underachievers, serve as appropriate guidelines for creating those classroom conditions and teaching methods which enable all pupils to advance according to their own needs and abilities.

EDUCATIONAL OBJECTIVES

1. Motivational

Enhance intrinsic motivation.
Provide consistent and relevant feedback.

Provide ample acknowledgment of improvement.
Promote mastery, competence and self-evaluation.

2. *Scholastic and Intellectual*

Develop thinking skills and intellectual depth.
Create stimulating and intellectually challenging learning situations.

3. *Creative*

Develop creative thinking and creativity in writing and the arts.
Provide opportunities for inquiry, self-initiateed learning and self-expression.
See Chapter 8 for a discussion of the creative process.

4. *Social*

Develop social skills, awareness and responsibility.
Provide educational experiences involving social interaction and social learning.

5. *Emotional*

Promote social adjustment and growth.
Create a supportive classroom climate and establish accepting and responsive relationships with the children.

In order to fulfil these objectives I designed an educational framework which could help teachers both to recognize individual needs and abilities and to provide appropriate educational practice which should enable underachievers and achieving pupils to advance according to their own needs and abilities. The following ideas were successfully introduced into different educational frameworks by teachers who participated in the intervention programme, by teachers in special classes for the gifted, and by myself.

CLASSROOM CLIMATE

The classroom climate is the creation of the teacher. Explicitly and implicitly it reflects the teacher's values, expectations, educational aims and her ability to establish accepting and supportive relationships between her and the children and among the class members. Particularly during the primary school stage, the classroom is the most appropriate place for the fulfilment of children's educationai needs.

The previous chapter highlighted the important role played by the teacher in fulfilling the emotional needs of the underachiever. Moreover, it showed that when children became more secure in their relations with the teacher, they began to benefit from the educational experiences provided both by the intervention programme and by the normal class situation. Thus, it seems important to create a classroom environment which encourages acceptance of children, provides support and promotes emotional well-being. The question arises—how can the teacher facilitate these processes?

1. CREATING A WELCOMING ENVIRONMENT

The first day of the school year offers a fresh start for every child and an opportunity to open a new page in his school life. A pleasant and welcoming classroom environment and stimulating activities can both alleviate the pupil's anxiety and raise his school expectations. The summer holidays provide teachers with a good opportunity for planning and structuring classroom environments, preparing materials and collecting and assembling items for display. The classroom should be both aesthetically attractive and stimulating. Indeed, the thought invested in its initial structure reflects the expectations of the teacher from her class and constitutes its 'hidden curriculum'. Thus, the teacher's acceptance of her class members can be communicated by sharing with them some of her special interests. By preparing an attractive display featuring items illustrating various aspects of her interests, the teacher is communicating to her pupils that they are worthy of her effort and that sharing personal interests is an important activity.

2. EASING THE HOLIDAY–SCHOOL TRANSFER

A useful way to welcome the pupils and ease the holiday–school transfer is to start the first day with an activity which enables children to share their holiday experiences with the teacher and the class members.

After introducing herself, the teacher can spend some time in describing her holiday experiences and special interests, and explaining the contents and nature of the display she has prepared for the class. This activity can be followed by asking the pupils to write an illustrated account of some of their holiday experiences to be shared with the class. Their contributions should be displayed in a previously prepared bright space. This experience enables the children to look back on their holidays and to look forward to sharing their interests with the teacher and class members, and provides the teacher with a good opportunity to encourage the children to plan and prepare their own interest corners for the class. Thus, as well as offering curriculum enrichment, it provides children with a sense of belonging, and sets the 'stage' for the creation of a congenial and stimulating class climate: while taking into account differences in structure of the secondary school, nonetheless this aspect is of equal importance to the secondary school learning situation. Thus the role of the classroom environment as a fundamental prerequisite of learning should be understood.

3. INTEGRATING ENVIRONMENTAL INTERESTS

The child's environment is an integral part of his life which should be integrated into the classroom. For some children the immediate environment would also have provided for holiday experiences. Thus, the initial introduction of the child to her classroom should include an attractive display of various aspects of environmental interest, such as local history, local architecture, the system of communication, places of interest and the people who live in the area. These features can be organized into various learning centres which serve a double purpose: (1) they convey to the pupils that the teacher is interested in the different aspects of their lives; (2) they provide a stimulating classroom environment capable of motivating the children to further study. Thus a shared involvement in environmental studies becomes part of the curriculum.

1. CREATING A RESPONSIVE CLASS CLIMATE

The behaviour of the teacher during the discussion on the different aspects of the environment displayed in the classroom can constitute an important factor in the shaping of a supportive and responsive class atmosphere. In encouraging the pupils to share their knowledge of their environment with the class and to suggest different aspects for further study, the teacher is both demonstrating her confidence in the children's ability and conveying to them that their ideas are accepted and respected. By personal example, the teacher is initiating supportive peer interaction processes.

2. FORMULATING A CODE FOR CLASSROOM BEHAVIOUR

A relevant extension of the discussion on the school's environment, previously mentioned, can be provided by an activity aimed at constructing a classroom code of behaviour which would be acceptable to all class members. This activity reinforces the children's sense of belonging, deepens their classroom involvement, and thus provides an appropriate ending to the first school day. This task involves emotional and intellectual processes and requires productive thinking which can be achieved by utilizing individual, group and class activities:

(1)   *Individual work:* Each child is asked to write the behaviours they like and dislike, and make suggestions for the class rules of behaviour.
(2)   *Group Work:* Every group discusses the individual suggestions, selecting those rules which are acceptable to the group members, and constructing their code of class behaviour.
(3)   *Class activity:* Following the presentation of the group's efforts, the whole class constructs a joint class code of behaviour.

The classroom code of behaviour can also include a section on desired teacher behaviour. I have discovered that when children and teachers become active participants in shaping classroom behavioural norms, they also feel responsible for maintaining the behavioural code and norms they have created.

Finally, it is important to emphasize that the above-mentioned suggestions can only serve as a productive beginning to the initiation of classroom processes capable of providing the continuous reinforcement and emotional support needed for achieving effective learning. Similar processes obtained by the intervention programme are described in Figure 4.4.

CLASSROOM STRUCTURE AND ORGANIZATION

In seeking to reduce and prevent underachievement, care must be taken to ensure that each pupil is making the progress that he is capable of. For this purpose, continuous processes of identification of children's abilities and needs and evaluation of their progress should constitute an integral part of the classroom structure. The following educational practices provide the teacher with effective tools to enable her to recognize her pupils' capabilities, weaknesses and strengths and to evaluate their scholastic performance.

1. CHILD–TEACHER EVALUATION MEETINGS

At the beginning of the school year the teacher initiates weekly personal meetings with every child. The first meeting should be devoted to getting to know the pupil, her interests, hobbies, scholastic strengths and weaknesses. The meeting is conducted in a free and friendly atmosphere and concluded with an explanation that the weekly meetings would give both pupil and teacher an opportunity to evaluate the child's school progress. The child is given a notebook in which to record her evaluation of her work in each subject by answering questions, according to the following diagnostic criteria. Simultaneously, the teacher keeps weekly records of these meetings. The child's weekly evaluation for each subject should cover:

(a) *Effort invested:*
'Have I invested enough effort in working on this subject during the week?'
(b) *Likes and dislikes:*
'What did I like best and what did I dislike doing in this subject during the week?'
(c) *Strengths and weaknesses:*
'Was the work too easy or too difficult?'
(d) *Personal choice:*
'What kind of work would I prefer to do?'

The pupil's answers to these questions constitute a continuous process of evaluation, enable the teacher to introduce and maintain systematic work habits and provide ample opportunities for guidance and encouragement.

2. PUPIL–TEACHER CONTRACT PROGRAMME

While the child–teacher weekly meetings provide general information and evaluation of the child's scholastic performance (for detailed description of the programme, see Chapters 5 and 6) the individual contract programme, described in previous chapters, enables pupil and teacher both to identify underachieving patterns of behaviour before they become deeply entrenched and to assume joint responsibility in planning appropriate experiences to alleviate problems and improve academic achievements.

The pupil–teacher meetings for the purpose of drawing up the contracts fulfil an important role in achieving the optimal development of every pupil and thus should become an integral part of classroom organization and structure. It is suggested that this programme should be introduced in the second month of the first term. As the programme develops, the teacher can conduct weekly meetings with those pupils who are either underachievers, or at risk of becoming so, while fortnightly meetings can be conducted with the remaining class members. This method enables the teacher to maintain continuous processes of identification of abilities and problems, initiate appropriate learning experiences, and establish a fruitful child−teacher partnership in working towards the common goal of the full realization of the potential of every child.

3. PERSONAL DIARY: BRIDGING THE HOME−SCHOOL GAP

Classroom organization should provide regular opportunities for bridging the home−school gap. In addition to various environmental activities, outlined previously, it is suggested that a daily period, preferably at the beginning of the school day, should be devoted to individual writing of diaries as an attractive personal book. This experience provides an immediate outlet for relating personally meaningful experiences, which often need processing prior to embarking on normal scholastic assignments. In addition, this activity fulfils several purposes:

(1)   Facilitating free expression.
(2)   Developing written communication skills.
(3)   Fostering creative writing.
(4)   Providing a deeper insight into children's lives and needs and opportunities for extending appropriate help and support.

The following example serves to illustrate some of these aspects.

A few days after I had taken my fifth-grade class to the Tate Gallery, one of my pupils described the visit in his diary. His account started with a factual description of the underground trip, the friends he sat with and the sweets they shared. Suddenly he began to describe in great detail one of Turner's paintings, depicting a cow emerging from a river. Apparently, this picture 'triggered off' meaningful associations of a frightening experience he had had, when, as a result of the ebbing tide, he had been marooned on a rock with his sister during a family outing.

This 'story' is a good example of the creative process, (see Chapter 8) and demonstrates the need to provide opportunities for incorporating home and out-of-school experiences into the normal classroom structure.

4. INDIVIDUAL FILES: ENABLING CONTINUOUS ASSESSMENT

Compiling individual files for every child constitutes an effective method for maintaining the process of continuous assessment. Each file contains information revealed by the child−teacher evaluation meetings, examples of the pupil's work in all the scholastic and creative fields which should be collected regularly, examples of tests taken and examination results. The file's contents serve as a productive basis for joint child−teacher and child−teacher−parents evaluation sessions which provide a good opportunity for feedback, reinforcement and guidance.

CURRICULUM WORK AND ENRICHMENT

Systematic curriculum work in the basic subjects should constitute an integral part of the pupil's school day. However, in order to ensure that every child is sufficiently 'stretched' a differentiated curricula should be introduced to meet the wide range of needs and aptitudes of the pupils. A differentiated curricula should provide all the class members with the appropriate stimulus and challenge required for all pupils to make the progress of which they are capable.

Since children vary in the knowledge they have in the different curricular areas and the level of their understanding of basic concepts and concept formation, the teacher should adopt a flexible approach by utilizing methods of class teaching, group work and individual learning to promote optimal learning.

Class teaching can be used for:

(1) Arousing curiosity and creating involvement in the subject or area to be learnt.
(2) Providing intellectual challenge.
(3) Fostering creative processes.
(4) Providing feedback and reinforcement.
(5) Revision and summary.

Group work fulfils both scholastic and social functions. Curriculum group work enables the children to learn from each other, and to join forces in dealing with more complex assignments, such as problem-solving in arithmetic and tasks requiring abstract thinking. This method provides the teacher with an appropriate educational situation for introducing new concepts and consolidating previous learning.

While there are different methods for grouping children, they all fulfil aims that must be understood by the pupils in order to enable them to benefit from the educational experiences provided by this method.

It is suggested that some time should be devoted to discussing the aims of group work and the appropriate behaviours required for achieving effective group learning. This discussion can be followed by the preparation of a chart for 'Group Work Rules' which must be observed. Systematic improvement in the quality of the processes of group learning can be achieved by attaching an 'observer' to each group who is responsible for evaluating the group's adherence to the behaviours and criteria required by the 'Class Group Work Rules'. The observations, which are recorded in a special book, can constitute a good basis for class discussion and evaluation. On every group work occasion, members of a different group act as observers.

Individual learning in every curriculum area fulfils several important needs:

(1) Self-regulation: each child can work according to his ability and regulate the effort needed to make good progress.

(2) Practising individual learning styles: children differ in their learning styles and need opportunities for choosing both the level and the style of learning.
(3) Obtaining individual help, guidance and feedback from the teacher.
(4) Facilitates the implementation of a differentiated curricula.

CURRICULUM ENRICHMENT

Stimulating curricula experiences should provide ample opportunities for curriculum enrichment. The school, the class, the teachers, the parents and the environment can provide different experiences and sources which can be utilized for the enrichment of the curriculum. For example, while talking to an Australian girl who joined the sixth-grade class, I discovered that she played the violin. She agreed to play for the class on the following Friday. Her excellent performance stimulated the initiation of several enrichment activities. First, in order to help her get used to our child-centred learning situation, which contrasted greatly with the formal school situation of her homeland, I suggested that she choose a musical aspect for her personal topic. She chose to study the development of different musical instruments. Several children became interested in this topic and joined her. This work developed into a variety of related interests, such as the structure and nature of different instruments, sound and vibration, musical styles and so on. Several corners were devoted to the display of written studies, books, models, paintings and charts. In addition, the class asked to form an orchestra. We collected and made percussion instruments, I taught the children to play the recorder and our new pupil made her unique contribution by playing the violin. Thus, our new class member was able both to ease her acclimatization process and to contribute to the enrichment of the class curriculum.

A different source for curriculum enrichment should be provided by teachers and parents' special interests, hobbies and expertise. Parents should be encouraged to share their interests and career experiences with the class and assume responsibility for conducting enrichment activities. In this connection mothers can play an important role. It will be remembered that underachieving girls who participated in the intervention programme expressed a much higher level of 'fear of success' reflecting their ambivalence towards academic success. This factor can explain the small proportion of girls attending special programmes for the gifted. Thus, it is most important to initiate enrichment activities which are concerned with the contribution that women can make to different areas and fields of knowledge. Mothers of children can be invited to talk about their professions and careers, and guest women lecturers can be invited to talk about their professional experiences. In addition, this aspect can be discussed during normal curriculum studies in literature, history and current affairs.

2. TEACHING METHODS

The following teaching methods have been designed to fulfil the educational aims previously outlined in this chapter. These methods were introduced and implemented successfully by teachers teaching in regular classes and special classes for gifted children, by receiving counselling from me, by teachers who participated in the intervention programme for underachievers, and by myself, while teaching primary school children in heterogeneous classes in London.

(a) PERSONAL PROJECTS

Objectives and implementation:

(1) *To cater for individual interests*
     Each child selects an individual topic, a personal interest, not necessarily connected with the curriculum. The research is conducted both in and out of school. For example, the topic: 'Six months in the development of my baby brother', which was selected by a fifth-grade girl, involved observations of her brother, a visit to a babies' home in town and in a kibbutz, and reading about the development of 6−12 month-old babies.

(2) *To develop thinking and systematic work habits*
     (a) Each child states, in writing, the reasons for choosing the topic.
     (b) Each child writes the questions that he would like to investigate and why. For example, in the project previously mentioned, the girl wrote that she wanted to find out how different aspects of the development of her baby brother compared with those of other babies of the same age.
     (c) Each child discovers and selects available resources for each question: bibliography, interviews, observations, and relevant visits.
     (d) The child presents each question as a chapter title, categorizes and lists suggested sources for each chapter.

(3) *Learning by inquiry*
     After consultation with the class teacher, the appropriate resources and tools are selected for each chapter. The adoption of research tools and methods of learning by inquiry are encouraged. For example:
     (a) The topic: 'Six months in the development of my baby brother': The girl conducted observations, discovered the norms for physical, cognitive, emotional and social development by means of reading and interviews with mothers and day-care personnel.
     (b) The topic on 'Astrology', introduced by a fifth-grade boy as a problem: 'My mother is interested in this topic, and believes in it. I want to discover whether the subject is scientific, or is just beliefs which have not been proven'.The problem was then subdivided into questions. Each question became a chapter and resources were stated. The child discovered various methods in order to verify the statements and calculations stated in the literature. The child tried to test his hypotheses and concluded that he was left with unsolved problems!
     (c) The topic: 'Photography', selected by a sixth-grade boy. The boy tested various hypotheses by experimental and discovery methods. Each chapter dealt with what happened under different conditions and the reason for the outcomes.

(4) *To develop creative thinking and creativity in various areas*
    (a) Alternative hypotheses are encouraged.
    (b) Various and different solutions are offered.
    (c) Creative methods of communication, display, demonstrations and use of materials are encouraged.

For example; in the topic: 'My family roots', the child traced, in a very imaginative way, three generations of his family, and discovered various original documents, school certificates, prices paid for articles and so on. Each question became a chapter in which the particular question was investigated as well as the different hypotheses concerning possible family developments as a result of alternative career and domicile choices. Finally the roots of the family and the links between the generations were presented by various creative modes of communication and display.

(5) *To develop social skills*
    (a) The pupils in the class share their experiences and discuss the various aspects of their study.
    (b) Children learn and practise the art of social communication.
    (c) Social topics which were chosen, offered an opportunity to get to know and understand children and people from different cultures.

For example; children in both primary and secondary schools selected topics which dealt with various historical and cultural aspects, concerned with the multicultural nature of the country they lived in.

Finally, it is important to emphasize that writing a personal project should be an integral part of each school year. Thus, it can provide a continuous process of fulfilling the educational objectives, as well as enabling children to acquire disciplined work habits needed for facilitating optimal development.

(b) Learning Centres

This method can be utilized for learning most of the curricular subjects.

(i) Initiation and implementation

The subject or area to be studied is divided into six to eight separate topics. Each topic becomes a comprehensive and self-sufficient learning centre, providing all the learning experiences needed for mastering the various aspects of the particular topic. Thus, each centre should include the following items and activities constituting a reusable pack:

(1) An introductory card, providing background knowledge, explaining the structure and contents of the centre—the assignments, resources and visual aids.
(2) A card providing the information needed for mastering the subject and concepts of the particular topic.
(3) Questions' Card.

(4) Answers' Card.
(5) Creative activities; for example: creating games, quizzes, writing a play, preparing a film, acting a relevant simulation play and so on.
(6) Enrichment material; for example: a box of relevant slides for self-viewing, newspaper clippings, documents, collection of drawings, enrichment books and so on.

Every topic has its set of cards. Cards should be large and attractive, and kept in a separate transparent envelope.

This method is most appropriate for group learning. It is suggested that a weekly double period be devoted to this activity. Every week the group completes one of the centres. In addition to the structured centres, the teacher can provide a 'free centre' including additional enrichment material to be used by group members who have completed the assignments.

This method of learning fulfils all the objectives outlined previously. In addition, it provides opportunities for non-competitive group cooperation, group problem-solving and the integration of fields of knowledge.

The following examples illustrate these aspects.

1. *Haifa, our city:* Fourth-grade learning centres integrating geography, history, archaeology and nature studies.

In addition to the activities involved in completing eight learning centres, several Saturday outings for parents, children and the teacher were devoted to first-hand discovery. All participants were divided into groups. Each group studied one important aspect or feature of the city and offered alternative solutions for solving the particular problems that were identified. The findings of all groups were discussed by the whole class on the completion of all the activities involved in these learning centres. Each group prepared a test for the class covering the aspects included in one learning centre.

2. *Egypt: Present and past:* Fifth grade learning centres integrating art, history, geography and current affairs.

In this case children's questions constituted the basis for planning centres in the different disciplines. For example, one pupil raised the question of the origin of the Egyptian writing system. The pupil's questions served for the planning of one centre incorporating activities and assignments needed for answering the child's questions:
The Centre: Egyptian Writing
The child's questions:

(1) How did the writing develop?
(2) How was it structured?
(3) What materials were used for writing?
(4) What was writing used for in those days?

(5) What did the ancient Egyptians write about?
(6) Did everybody know how to write?

A similar approach was used in the preparation of all the learning centres of this topic.

Learning centres can be prepared by the class teacher or a team of teachers, by groups of children or by an individual child. In addition, children can prepare learning centres based on their personal interests. These centres provide further enrichment for the class and enable the individual child to receive feedback and reinforcement both from the class members and from the teacher.

(c) Interdisciplinary studies

These provide excellent opportunities for introducing differentiated curricular experiences. In addition, an imaginative approach to the planning of interdisciplinary studies is conducive to fulfilling cognitive and social needs and can thus contribute both to raising scholastic standards in different subjects and to enhancing motivation for further study in favourite and less liked subjects.

This teaching method can be adopted for any combination of subjects and is appropriate for children of all abilities and age groups. The following example, prepared and implemented by a sixth-grade teacher in a Haifa school, could be adapted to different fields of knowledge:

Jerusalem: An interdisciplinary study

(1) *The stimulus: Creating involvement:*
     At the beginning of the school year the teacher suggested organizing a two-day trip to Jerusalem and asked the children to make suggestions for planning the trip.
(2) *Challenging points of departure:*
     Children's suggestions of visits to places of interests and areas needed investigation prior to the trip to Jerusalem and constituted fruitful points of departure in planning the study.

     Following this discussion the teacher prepared a chart which included all the important factors which are reflected in the city today. Several challenging and introductory talks concerned with the different aspects of the history, geography, and religions of the city were given by the teacher in order to provide background knowledge required for the choice of topics by the children.
(3) *Interdisciplinary approach: differentiated curricula:*
     Each child selected an area for interdisciplinary study, such as a period in the history of Jerusalem, a geographical area, Jerusalem reflected by its holy places, Jerusalem as reflected in the Bible, water systems and problems through the ages, Jerusalem as a spiritual centre and so on. The children consulted the teacher on the availability of sources and the scope of the study. Children were asked to formulate one central question and to attempt to answer it, using all the resources available.

The topics were written up in the form of attractive books and presented to the whole class.

(4) *Jerusalem reflected in the literature: a class activity:*
Class visits to the school and university libraries were devoted to discovering the literature and poetry concerned with Jerusalem. Every child selected one of these works for personal reading. Some class lessons were devoted to a study in depth of some of the literature. In addition, children prepared talks on the works they had read and liked.

(5) *The trip to Jerusalem: consolidating knowledge, widening horizons, fostering social relationships:*
(1) Preparations for the trip:
The class was organized into groups of four children, due to the seating arrangements in the bus. Each group was asked to prepare a contribution to the social event, to select a place of interest that they would like to visit and to equip the group with a map, a geography book, a notebook and a pen.
(2) The two-hour drive to Jerusalem was devoted to a group activity:
All groups received 10 questions to answer, each question relating to one of the places passed on route. Each group noted these places on their map and evaluated their answers. Prizes and consolation prizes were given by the teacher at the social evening which took place in Jerusalem.
(6) *Concluding the study: A creative approach*
On returning from the trip every group prepared a creative presentation of one interesting experience, aspect or event associated with their visit, such as a play, a painting, a model etc. Finally all children's individual studies and group creative efforts were displayed attractively in an exhibition.

(d) Help club: Peer tutorship

This idea was first suggested by an underachieving pupil who participated in the intervention programme and it was subsequently implemented by his teacher. This method enables children both to be helped by and to offer help to their class members.

(i) Implementation

(1) *Listing offered help.*
One pupil assumes responsibility for compiling a catalogue of names of children offering help and the subject, skill or area in which help is offered.
(2) *Listing required help.*
Another pupil assumes responsibility for the listing and cataloguing of names of children seeking help and the subjects or skills requiring help.
Care must be taken to include every child in both lists.

(3)   *Keeping records.*
An attractive corner can be devoted to the activities of the help club. The corner should include both catalogues. Children should be encouraged to make a note in the appropriate record book of the help they offered or received. The teacher should take an interest in these activities, offer encouragement and support.

The 'help club' provides the teacher with an additional tool which enables the gaining of further insight into children's scholastic problems and scholastic strengths, and thus provides further opportunities for the planning of appropriate learning experiences. Moreover, although this activity was originally created by a gifted underachiever in order to cater for specific needs (see Chapter 8) it generally fulfils the important needs for enhancing children's self-image, recognition of mastery and competence, raising one's social status and developing scholastic and social skills.

In conclusion, I hope that the educational practices which I have outlined in this chapter will help the school's educational staff to plan and create appropriate educational environments, making it possible for all pupils to advance, according to their own needs and abilities, thus contributing to the reduction and eventual prevention of underachievement.

CHAPTER 8

Teaching the Gifted Underachiever

This chapter will be concerned with the characteristics and educational needs of gifted underachieving children. While the procedures for identification and educational practice discussed in Chapter 7 are appropriate for underachievers of all levels of ability, Chapter 6 revealed that gifted underachievers expressed a greater need for a self-directed and creative style of learning. This chapter will provide teachers both with an understanding of the creative process and with ideas for creative educational practice appropriate for teaching the gifted underachiever. Finally, the specific educational needs of gifted underachieving girls will be discussed.

Chapters 4 and 6 have clearly demonstrated that underachievers of high intellectual abilities found it more difficult to adjust to the norms and requirements of the normal classroom situation. Since the adaptive problems of the gifted underachiever often stem from specific personality and learning styles which are not always understood by the teacher, they merit separate consideration.

THE PROBLEM OF IDENTIFICATION

It seems surprising that in a culture that believes in the right of the individual to fully develop his unique talents and in a society which values education for all and maintains prolonged compulsory education, the needs of the gifted child are not yet fully met (Raph, Goldberg and Passow, 1966). Furthermore, despite the increasing interest in gifted education stimulated by the growing need to meet the scientific and technological challenges of the space era, very little attention has been directed to the gifted underachiever (Waddington and O'Brien, 1979; Freeman, 1979; Davis and Rimm, 1985; Gallagher, 1985). The reason for this neglect seems to lie in the difficulties encountered by teachers in recognizing ability in the young child, when it is not manifested in normal convergent school behaviour. The seriousness of the problem was demonstrated by an example given by Tempest (1974) of two children who were not recognized as gifted by their teachers, although their reading age, as measured by the Schonell Word Recognition Test, was six years above their chronological age.

It is understandable that it is more difficult to recognize high intellectual ability in the young child who 'chooses', for various reasons (see Chapter 2) to hide her ability by complying only to the minimal daily school requirements. While such patterns of behaviour may have originated at home, their persistent manifestation in school probably reflect the child's growing boredom and frustration in class.

The gifted child's ability to perceive his problems, his critical awareness of his own inadequate performance as well as recognition of the failure of the educational environment to satisfy his needs may lead to behavioural and emotional problems. Since inadequate emotional adjustment frequently interferes with the ability of teachers to recognize scholastic capacity (Kellmer-Pringle, 1970; Whitmore, 1980) teachers should become familiar with behavioural manifestations which characterize the gifted underachiever. The following characteristics should help the teacher to identify these children in class.

1. CHARACTERISTICS OF GIFTED UNDERACHIEVERS

Whitmore (1980), who summarized some of the most important traits of gifted under-achievers, suggested that if a child who has wide general knowledge, great 'expertise' in a specific hobby or interest or a lively imagination and creative ability, also manifests ten or more of the following characteristics the teacher should initiate evaluative procedures in order to determine whether the child is a gifted under-achiever (see Chapter 7 for identification and evaluation methods).

(1)   Large gap between quality of oral and written work.
(2)   Failure to complete daily school work.
(3)   Poor execution of work.
(4)   Persistent dissatisfaction with accomplishments.
(5)   Avoidance of trying new activities.
(6)   Low self-image.
(7)   Aggressive behaviour.
(8)   Does not function well in a group situation.
(9)   Lacks concentration.
(10) Sets unrealistic self-expectations (goals too low or too high).
(11) Difficulty in peer relationships.
(12) Poor attitudes to school.
(13) Dislikes drill and memorization.

These characteristics reflect the emotional, social, scholastic and creative needs which were observed and reported by teachers in Chapter 6. While they serve to emphasize that the achievement of emotional well-being constitutes an essential prerequisite for attaining effective learning, they also suggest that gifted children have difficulties in conforming to restrictive classroom procedures such as repetitive work, rote learning and passive listening to the teacher. Acceptance of and adjustment to convergent classroom norms are particularly difficult for the creative gifted child who is characterized by an associative divergent thinking style which thrives on self-initiated inquiry, freedom of choice of assignments and stimulating open-ended learning experiences. When children are given these opportunities, they frequently widen the scope of their learning, initiate further inquiry and engage in a more

118

problem-orientated approach. Furthermore, they often select original methods of presenting their work. Such behaviours reflect the need for a more personal and creative style of learning. Though the need to foster creativity in children is generally recognized, the processes involved, in terms of classroom environment and practice, are not always understood. In view of the complex nature of the creative act, some clarification of the role it plays in the child's development should be helpful.

THE CREATIVE PROCESS

Any creative activity is an expression of intellectual and emotional needs. The 'finished' product—the story, the painting, the solved problem—is the integration of such needs. For example, a child's immediate emotional state, such as anxiety or unhappiness, and his need to clarify ideas or feelings determine the choice of experiences to be related and the choice of medium most appropriate for expressing these immediate needs. The stimuli that a child receives help him to form concepts. First- and second-hand experiences enable the widening of one's field of experiences and the shaping of patterns and relationships needed for the clarification of ideas and the processing of feelings. For example, a girl in an infant school drew a picture of her family. In response to the teacher's question: 'Where is your brother?', she answered: 'He always annoys me—I am fed up with him'. In this case, the girl expressed her frustration by 'expelling' the brother from the family nest. The complex role of the creative activity in helping children to clarify ideas is expressed in the following poem written by a fourth-grade gifted underachiever. The poem, written in Hebrew, is presented in its literal translation:

A Dream
A dream is a thing that fulfils dreams,
A dream cannot be seen,
It is a feeling.
A dream is a voice—
—a gentle murmur of sadness or joy.

The dream tells of itself
The dream repeats our yesterdays,
The dream is in my heart,
The dream is about me,
The dream is a real thing!

The urge to express both cognitive and emotional needs is revealed in the following drawing which was given to me by a thirteen-year-old underachiever in a London School. This picture is a good example of the integration of first-hand experiences—in this case, the school and home environment—and second-hand experiences—knowledge of prehistoric monsters derived from books. These images were chosen by this boy to help clarify certain aspects of his environment and to express his strong feelings of frustration towards his environment.

Figure 8.1   The Monster from the Earth: The Creative Product

In order to enable children to develop creative abilities they need stimulating experiences and a classroom situation which is conducive to fostering creative processes. The teacher can play an important role by maintaining the following conditions:

(1) *Receptivity and openness:*
     to ideas stemming from the pupils;
     to one's own ideas;
     to ideas from other sources.

(2) *Incubation:*
     Allowing for time to form free and personal associations. For example, not to require a written response after every given stimulus.

(3) *Freedom:*
     Allowing freedom of choice in selection of assignments, topics and medium of expression. This aspect was illustrated in all the examples previously mentioned.

(4) *Absence of external evaluation:*
     Since the creative activity should express personal needs, care must be taken not to apply external criteria of evaluation to the creative products of children.

EDUCATIONAL EXPERIENCES FOR GIFTED UNDERACHIEVERS

The following activities fulfil intellectual, social and emotional needs which are important for underachievers and achievers of all ability levels. The specific needs of the creative gifted underachievers can be expressed in the end-products.

1. UTILIZING MASS MEDIA

Television programmes and newspapers can provide productive sources for creative educational experiences. Since gifted underachievers tend to spend more time watching television and reading newspapers as these activities postpone the fulfilling of less desirable obligations—such as school work—they can constitute appropriate starting points for various creative learning experiences.

The following activities can be extended to different curricula areas. In addition to fulfilling the educational needs discussed above, they should motivate the gifted child to produce written work—which gifted children in general (Freeman, 1979) and gifted underachievers in particular (Whitmore, 1980; Butler-Por, 1982) are reluctant to do.

(a) Creating television programmes

(1) Children select a television programme in an area in which they are interested.

(2) Following a class discussion on formulation of criteria for evaluation, each child formulates her own criteria and evaluates the programme accordingly.

(3)   Working individually or in pairs, children formulate alternative criteria as a basis for creating their own new programme.
(4)   Children write their programmes, select their players and together prepare the costumes, and stage props and designs.
(5)   The plays are produced. Parents, television producers of the original programmes and other classes are invited.

(b) Writing and editing a newspaper

(1)   Class visit to a newspaper editor, followed by a discussion on the various aspects of the newspaper industry.
(2)   Children choose the type of newspaper they would like to produce—a weekly class newspaper, a monthly school one, or a journal devoted to an area in which they are interested.
(3)   Children can work individually, in pairs or groups. They take turns in assuming responsibility for editing and producing the newspaper.

(c) Mass media as sources for developing personal projects

The following activities provide an alternative method to the learning centres described in Chapter 7. The flexible interdisciplinary nature of this approach can be utilized for productive learning in every curriculum area. The specific example which follows demonstrates the importance of a teacher's acceptance of children's interests, openness to ideas and willingness to provide her pupils with a good example of creative learning.

LEARNING CENTRES, AN INTEGRATIVE APPROACH
An example of a Centre on Italy

Background
Generally, learning centres dealing with various aspects of Italy constitute both an appropriate and a productive field of inquiry, since the interest of many children is stimulated by visits to the country and by the mass media. Specifically, several underachievers selected this country as a result of their interest in Italy stimulated by their recent holiday there. The method employed by the children was based, as described in Chapters 6 and 7, on the questions and issues they were interested in investigating.
  The following example is a teacher's contribution to the class interest in Italy. The method can be used in a variety of subjects. The material, structure and questions for such learning centres can be prepared by the pupils.

Method
(1)   *Collection of data*
      Two to three weeks are devoted to collecting articles, news items, visual material from newspapers and summaries from relevant radio and television programmes concerning the topic selected, in this case Italy.

(2) *Formulating questions for study*
First the material is read and categorized. Subsequently, it is organized in subtitles. Each item is named and pasted on manila paper. Each subtitle constitutes a learning centre. Questions are formulated and written underneath the picture or article.

(3) *Study and creative work*
When centres are completed, children can work in groups or individually at each centre separately, devoting 1–2 hours for each centre.

Centre 1—Volcanoes in Italy

Card 1: The structure of volcanoes
Sources: Newspaper reports on a current volcanic threat.
Questions:

(1) What do you know about volcanic eruptions?
(2) How is a volcanic mountain formed?
(3) Draw a volcanic mountain and specify its components.
(4) Which functions are fulfilled by the components of the volcanic mountain?
(5) What types of volcanic mountains do you know? Can you categorize them?
(6) Can you tell us of other eruptions you have heard or read about?
(7) Write an imaginative story or poem about a volcanic eruption.

Card 2: Preservation of Pompeii
Sources: A newspaper picture of ancient Pompeii and a report of a historical description of the occurrence.
Questions:

(1) What have you learnt from this description of the ancient city of Pompeii and the actual eruption?
(2) What reasons accounted for the preservation of Pompeii?
(3) Write a story, a poem, or play describing what happened and the feelings of an eye witness.
(4) Make a model or draw a picture of ancient Pompeii.

Card 3: Pompeii Reflected in the Literature
Sources: A contemporary poem.
Questions:

(1) What can you learn about Pompeii from this poem?
(2) Can you find other stories or poems on Pompeii?

Centre 2—Venice

Card 1: Venice is sinking
Sources: Newspaper reports and photos of sinking Venice, and the dam.

Questions:

(1)   What are the dangers threatening Venice?
(2)   What effects can these problems have on the people of Venice?
(3)   How can the dam save Venice?
(4)   What alternative methods can stop the sinking of Venice?

Card 2: Venice in art and literature
Sources: Two poems, including Bertinni's, on Venice. Collection of cards of the art of Venice. Class visit to a museum to see Venetian art.
Questions:

(1)   Which poem did you like best and why?
(2)   Which painting did you like best and why?
(3)   Have you been to Venice? If so, what did you like best?
(4)   What can you learn about life in Venice from the paintings you have seen in the museum?

Centre 3—Agriculture in Italy

Card 1: Products
Sources: Newspaper clippings of *Cheese Bank in Italy*, wine production, article on agriculture in Italy and its marketing.
Questions:

(1)   The Cheese Bank—is it a good solution for solving the economic distress of Italian farmers? Can you think of alternative methods?
(2)   What can you learn from the photo of wines about the wines of Italy? What else do you know about wine production in Italy?
(3)   Look at the physical and climatic maps of Italy in the atlas. What can you learn about its climate and how does it affect its agriculture?
(4)   Have you any suggestions for improving the agricultural situation in Italy?

Centre 4—Industry in Italy

Card 1: The car industry
Sources: Newspaper photos and reports on the Italian car industry.
Questions:

(1)   What can you learn from these newspaper articles and photos about the car industry?
(2)   Compare the Italian models you know to others.

Card 2: Exports
Sources: A brief survey of Italian industry today, derived from a television programme, and newspaper items on Italian exports. Pictures of the fashion and leather industries.

Questions:

(1)   What can you learn from these items?
(2)   What are the reasons for immigration from south to north of Italy? How do they affect industrial developments in Italy?
(3)   How does urban industry affect its population?
(4)   What does Italy Export?
(5)   Compare the fashions in these pictures to those you see in shops. Which ones do you like best and why?

Centre 5—Tourism

Card 1: Places of interest
Sources: Magazine pictures and articles of Italian towns and resorts, postcards.
Questions:

(1)   What can you learn from these pictures?
(2)   Have you been to or heard of any of these places?
(3)   Why do you think Italy attracts tourists all the year round?
(4)   Make a model, a plan, or a picture of your ideal tourist place.

Centre 6—Art in Italy

Card 1: Artistic interests
Sources: Art in Italy, pictures, newspaper articles of the opera and museum exhibitions.
Questions:

(1)   What are the advantages that Italy can offer to tourists?

Card 2: Art and science
Sources: Newspaper illustrated article on Leonardo da Vinci the artist and scientist.
Questions:

(1)   What can you learn about Leonardo da Vinci from the article and the paintings?
(2)   Art and science—can they be reconciled?

Card 3: Michelangelo
Sources: Photographs of Michelangelo's sculptures of Moses and David.
Questions:

(1)   Can you learn from the sculpture of Moses how Michelangelo perceived him? How would you describe Moses the Man?
(2)   Is Michelangelo's image of King David similar to that described in the Bible?

Centre 7—The Vatican

Card 1: A great religious centre

Sources: Newspaper reports, clippings and photos of the Vatican, and the Pope's recent activities.
Questions:

(1) What can you learn from these items of the reasons for the interest in the Vatican?
(2) What are the functions of the Pope and the reasons for his popularity?
(3) Can you think of the advantages and disadvantages of modernizing religious practices?

Centre 8—Ecological Aspects

Card 1: Pollution in sea resorts
Sources: Newspaper articles and photos of polluted sea resorts.
Questions:

(1) What are the reasons for the pollution you can see in these photos? What can be done to solve this problem?
(2) Have you seen this kind of pollution in our coasts? How can this problem be avoided?

Card 2: Urban neglect
Sources: Summary of television programme on some urban dirt and neglect in Italy.
Questions:

(1) How can one fight urban dirt and neglect?
(2) What other ecological hazards affect large cities? How can one reduce ecological hazards?

DEVELOPING SOCIAL SKILLS AND RESPONSIBILITY

As we have seen, the developing of social relationships and skills is problematic for gifted underachievers. The following learning experiences facilitate meaningful social interaction and contribute to the pupils' self-confidence and sense of belonging to the school and home environment.

1. SCHOOL TUTORSHIP SCHEME

An interesting extension of the peer-tutorship scheme, mentioned above, can be obtained by the introduction of an all-school tutorship scheme. The tutorship scheme provides individual tutoring of younger children by older children.

A weekly period can be devoted to a meeting of the young child with her tutor. These meetings can be either structured or unstructured. For, example, a structured tutorship programme which I designed, involving a secondary school class of gifted 14 year-old pupils in tutoring fourth grade gifted disadvantaged children, can be conducted within the primary school. The weekly two-hour meeting was devoted to the following activities:

(1) *Work on personal topic: 45 minutes*
     Each tutor chose, together with his pupil, a personal topic. Together they studied the topic and compiled a topic book.
(2) *Story reading of the tutor to the 'pupil': 15 minutes*
(3) *Games—playing together in small groups and making new games: 60 minutes.*

The structure and contents of the tutorship meeting can, of course, be adapted to the specific needs of the children. However, my experience has shown that both structured and unstructured tutorship programmes are capable of providing both the tutor and the tutored with educational experiences answering different motivational, scholastic and emotional needs, as well as creating meaningful interaction. Finally, it provides a good opportunity for education towards the development of personal responsibility and social awareness.

2. CHILDREN–PARENTS PARTNERSHIP IN LEARNING

Increasing parents' interest and involvement in their children's scholastic performance and school life can contribute greatly to reducing and preventing underachieving patterns of behaviour. However, far too often, parents express their interest in the child's scholastic progress by exercising excessive pressure or expressing feelings of anxiety and dissatisfaction with the child's scholastic achievements.

The following methods provide a good opportunity to deepen parents' involvement in their children's learning by creating a non-judgmental partnership between the children and their parents by involving them in a shared learning experience.

In order to achieve this objective I designed the following programme which can be adapted to any area of investigation. Though this particular programme was concerned with the study of the residential areas of school children attending schools in Haifa, it can of course be utilized in different areas.

STUDYING OUR ENVIRONMENT: CHILDREN–PARENTS COOPERATION
Implementation
(1) *Selecting topics for investigation*
     The teacher arranges a joint meeting for parents and pupils. The children and parents are asked to sit in neighbourhood groups. After a brief explanation of the purpose and nature of the activity, emphasizing that the children and parents are equal partners, the teacher provides each group with paper and pen and asks the groups to decide and list the questions that they would like to investigate in their residential environment. A period of approximately 30 minutes should be devoted to this activity.
(2) *Sharing ideas*
     Each group is asked to select one member, either child or parent, to list on the blackboard the group's questions selected for study. This activity provides opportunities for cross-fertilization.

(3) *Procedure: Bridging the home—school gap*
The teacher outlines the procedure for this activity which will include:

1: Neighbourhood children—parents' group study.
2: School presentation of group's investigations.

Each group is asked to decide on the first group learning meeting, which will take place in one of their homes. During the first meeting the group will set a time-table for their future meetings and plan the contents and structure of their study.

Monthly class meetings will be convened at school so that each group can present the results of their investigations. These findings can be communicated by different methods, thus providing opportunities for shared creative experiences of both children and parents. These class meetings motivated some groups to invite the whole class to share an experience or visit a place of interest in their neighbourhood.

The above approach can be most productive for investigating different areas of interest. Ecological problems, current affairs and future studies are particularly appropriate.

GIFTED GIRL UNDERACHIEVERS

It is unfortunate that on the whole parents seem to be satisfied with their daughters' school achievement even if they suspect that they could do much better and are not really investing sufficient effort in their work. The lower expectations from and aspirations of parents for their daughters are usually coupled with differential scholastic reinforcement given either covertly or overtly. For example, at a parents' meeting prior to enrolment for a class for highly gifted primary school children, one mother said that her daughter would stay in her present school as she was happy there and had many friends. The same mother approached me anxiously two years later, asking why her younger son had not yet been tested at school for eligibility for the same programme. Similarly, in a cross-cultural study of values considered important for boys and girls in Israel, I found that without exception parents and children coded scholastic and occupational achievement-oriented values much more highly for boys that for girls. These traditional sex role perceptions were also prevalent among the kibbutz populations, revealing the discrepancy between the ideology of equality between the sexes and actual value-related behaviour (Butler-Por, 1985). Such sex-related attitudes towards achievement explain the lower proportion of girls participating in programmes for gifted children and add understanding of the ambivalence felt by women and girls towards academic and career success, discussed in Chapter 2 (Horner, 1968; Butler and Nisan, 1975). The sex inequities expressed in socialization as well as societal sex role stereotyping, sex bias and discrimination (Carrelli, 1981) contribute to the development and practice of underachievement in the female child population.

CHARACTERISTICS

While generally the traits of gifted underachievers, described above, are also characteristics of gifted underachieving girls, the sex differentiation made by parents in the toys that they give their children, in the stories they read to them and in the books they buy for them, shape their cultural-oriented behaviour.

The reinforcement only of social behaviour, conformity, docility, as well as sex role characteristics of love of children, gentleness, compassion, affection, understanding and shyness, identified by Bem (1974), may well help initiate them into an underachieving role in society (Davis and Rimm, 1985).

In order to combat such tendencies, teachers should provide specific learning experiences which aim to raise the scholastic expectations and professional aspirations of their female pupils.

EDUCATIONAL EXPERIENCES

1. ALLEVIATING THE HOME–CAREER CONFLICT

As we have seen in Chapter 2, gifted girls often fear that academic and professional success is not compatible with femininity, social success and marriage. In order to reduce ambivalent feelings towards success, girls need to meet women who successfully combine a family and professional life.

The following suggestions should be helpful:

(1) The teacher compiles a list of parents' occupations and careers.
(2) Parents are invited to give a talk to the class on their work, the qualifications needed and responsibilities fulfilled.
(3) Mothers are asked to discuss their motivation for choice of profession, the posts of responsibility they hold and the aspects of self-fulfilment and its contribution to the life of the family.
(4) Class visits to parents' work places, followed by class discussion of the concept and practice of sex role stereotyping in career and professional choice.
(5) Girls are encouraged to prepare a project on one of the professional occupations described by the mothers, to be subsequently discussed and displayed in class.

2. FEMALE MODELS FOR IDENTIFICATION

Female models for identification can be found in literature, history, local and national government, the medical profession and institutes of higher education, industry and the arts.

(a) Literature

Teachers should include in the class library fiction books and biographies of women who became famous as a result of their contribution to society. It is advisable to exclude books which are strongly sex biased.

(b) History

Curriculum and enrichment activities should include learning experiences which emphasize the role played by women in shaping historical events. Discussion of these events, simulation games, and individual projects are most appropriate.

(c) Famous contemporary women

Local and national women who have attained a high level of achievement in any realm of endeavour are invited to share their experiences with the class children. In addition, girls are encouraged to interview those who cannot come to the school on the various aspects of their work and how it affects their personal life. Also the roles of internationally famous women should be discussed.

3. CREATIVE LEARNING EXPERIENCE

Creative activities such as creative writing, art and drama can help girls to understand their feelings and thoughts about their future roles and lives. In addition, the processes involved in the creative activity, as we have seen above, fulfil immediate emotional needs which for underachieving gifted girls may include the alleviation of feelings of frustration caused by unrealized potential resulting from their inability to satisfy their conflicting intellectual and social needs.

4. TEACHER SUPPORT

It is important to emphasize that the teacher can play a significant role in raising the academic self-concept of the underachieving girl by expressing confidence in her ability and encouraging her to undertaking challenging assignments of increasing complexity.

The successful completion of the various learning experiences and assignments, amply reinforced by the teacher, should help the girls to raise their own academic expectations as well as those of their parents and peers.

Finally, in order to reduce the scope of cultural underachievement among the female child population, educational efforts should be coupled with attitudinal changes in society.

CHAPTER 9

Implications for Teacher Education

This chapter will discuss the role that can be played by Institutes of Teacher Education in preparing students and teachers to cope effectively with underachievers in school. Two new models for Teacher Education will be described and discussed. These programmes, which proved successful in enhancing the understanding of students and teachers of the problems of underachievers and in providing educational methods needed for effective intervention, can be relevant for both pre- and in-service training of teachers.

One of the most encouraging aspects of the intervention programme for primary school underachievers, introduced and discussed in previous chapters, has been its effectiveness in producing positive educational changes both in the children and in the teachers who were involved with the programme. The question arises—which features in this programme can explain these effects? This aspect is of particular relevance for teacher education since it is often asked why changes in teachers' behaviour and in the improving of teaching seem so slow, despite the efforts which are invested in both teachers' pre-service and in-service training (Goodlad, 1970).

The answer to this question seems to be found in factors inherent in the change process which, according to Kurt Lewin (1948), requires three stages:

First—cognitive processing of change content
Second—internalization of content.
Third—change in behaviour which occurs on completion of the two stages.

When one considers these processes in terms of the structuring of teacher education courses, it seems possible to argue that though the knowledge gained through lectures and reading can help students and practising teachers understand the issues explaining a particular problem, no internalization and subsequent change in behaviour can take place unless the student-teacher and practising teacher can recognize the relevance of the knowledge gained by means of first-hand experiences in the actual school situation which necessitates solving specific problems which arise. It seems that the significant changes that occurred in the classroom behaviour of the teachers who participated in the intervention can be explained by their awareness that the programme offered relevant solutions to the problems encountered in school. Moreover, the integrative nature of the programme provided ample opportunities to examine and test the relevance of the theoretical aspects that were studied to the understanding of the problems of their pupils.

In view of the complex nature of underachievement and the need to prepare student-teachers and practising teachers to cope with this problem in school, it is believed that specific courses concerned with underachievement should be provided at both the pre- and in-service levels of teacher education which would aim to integrate theory and practice by providing meaningful and personal learning experiences which would facilitate the internalization of these experiences, thus paving the way for appropriate changes in classroom behaviour. By integrating such courses into the curriculum of teacher education, schools of education and teacher centres can play an important role in providing schools with the help needed to cope with one of the most serious problems facing education today—the failure of many pupils to reach the scholastic achievements of which they are capable.

Since the problem of underachievement concerns all schools and the whole school, the methods of dealing with it should concern all those responsible for the school. In this connection, it is important and relevant to note the recommendations of the Thomas Committee Report on Improving Primary Schools (1984):

> Every primary school should formulate a development plan in agreement with its governing body and the divisional primary school inspector. The plan should be a whole plan and show how the various advisory teachers on the staff will contribute. It should include an estimated time-scale and identify any resources required for its operation, including programmes of visits to other schools, attendance at courses, the employment of external advisory teachers or other support services. (3:82)

It seems appropriate that the school development plan should be concerned with formulating an in-service programme for their teachers aimed at helping them to cope effectively with underachieving children, employing the support services of teacher centres and schools of education.

The following models were designed to meet these needs by providing student-teachers and practising teachers with the learning experiences and teaching methods found to be effective in reducing underachievement in schools.

IN–SERVICE TEACHER TRAINING PROGRAMME FOR PRIMARY SCHOOL UNDERACHIEVERS

Teacher centres and institutes of higher education constitute productive frameworks for conducting integrative in-service courses aimed at providing teachers with the appropriate tools needed for helping their underachieving pupils. Thus a group of teachers, coming as they do for the purpose of an in-service course from different schools, bringing with them diverse experiences of underachieving children, can become a fruitful source for knowledge derived from first-hand experiences and an ideal setting for cooperative problem-solving, formulation of educational objectives and teaching methods conducive to improving the educational environment of underachievers.

1. INSTRUCTION AND SOURCE MATERIALS

The course can be conducted by educational advisers, school psychologists or school counsellors, who by definition can fulfil a double role: first to provide an educationally meaningful course and appropriate intervention tools, second to increase the school's awareness of the problem. In addition, they can help head teachers in the selection of course participants, which should include senior teachers who could assume subsequent responsibility for helping the school staff initiate intervention programmes for their underachievers.

While Chapters 1 and 2 should be helpful in planning the theoretical curriculum of the course and providing a reading source and bibliography for the participants, Chapters 5–7 offer a structured and practical education plan for the treatment and prevention of underachievement, which can be introduced fairly easily by teachers into the normal classroom situation.

2. OBJECTIVES

General: To develop a greater understanding of the problems and needs of underachieving children.

Specific:
(1) To provide the theoretical background needed to foster understanding of the origins of underachievement, the characteristics and educational difficulties of underachievers.
(2) To introduce teachers to the skills and teaching methods which will enable them to identify underachieving pupils.
(3) To offer practical help in conducting an effective intervention programme with their underachieving pupils.
(4) To provide on-going guidance in creating appropriate learning experiences conducive to reducing underachievement in school.

3. CURRICULUM

(a) Theoretical issues: Lectures and discussions

(1) Who is an underachiever?
(2) How can we identify underachievers of different levels of ability?
(3) Factors influencing underachievement.
    (i) personality characteristics:
        self-concept;
        fear of failure;
        fear of success;
        need affiliation
    (ii) Parental, cultural and societal factors:
        home climate, norms and expectations;
        the differently cultured underachiever;
        girl underachievers.

(iii) School factors:
classroom climate;
the role of intrinsic motivation;
the importance of reinforcement, feedback and teacher-pupil interaction;
teaching methods;
teacher attitudes and expectations.

(b) Educational practice: Workshop

(1) Educational strategies for alleviating underachievers' behavioural and learning difficulties.
(2) On-going guidance in the initiation and implementation of intervention treatment with underachieving children of superior and average ability.

4. PROCEDURE

Twelve weekly meetings. Each meeting lasting two to three hours, consisting of two parts:

(1) *Theory: 1 hour*
Discussion of theoretical issues explaining the origins and behaviours of underachievers.
(2) *Educational practice: Workshop 1—2 hours*
Teachers' reporting and discussing their work with their underachievers and receiving the tools and guidance for further intervention.

5. INTRODUCING THE COURSE—IMPLEMENTATION

First, it is important to establish a frame of reference for the course participants which will be purposeful enough to provide the theoretical understanding of the problem of underachievement and flexible enough for encouraging active participation of the teachers in sharing their experiences and problems with the course participants. Thus, at the beginning of the first meeting, the objectives of the course are explained, emphasizing the problematic nature of underachievement and the fact that although some of the reasons for the behaviour of underachievers are to be found outside the school, much can be done by the teachers within the classroom situation to alleviate the problems and improve the school performance of these children. Furthermore, during the course they will be provided with practical guidance on how to help their underachievers overcome their problems. Subsequently, some of the behavioural patterns of underachievers will be described followed by a discussion of the reasons that might explain these behaviours.

During the second part of the meeting, teachers are asked to introduce themselves and to describe one of their pupils who appears to be an underachiever.

At the end of the meeting, teachers are asked to try to identify two of their pupils who seem to be capable of better school performance than they have achieved, utilizing the following diagnostic methods described in detail in Chapter 7.

134

(1)   Evaluative class assignment
First the whole class is asked to write answers to the following questions:
   (a)   Effort invested
        'Have I invested enough effort in school work during the last week?'
        'Could I do better than I have done?'
   (b)   Likes and dislikes
        'Which activities did I like best and what did I dislike doing during the week?'
(c)   Strengths and weaknesses
'Was the work too easy or too difficult?'
(d)   Personal choice
'What kind of work that I have not done, would I like to do?'

The pupils' answers to these questions enable the teacher to discover possible patterns of underachievement and constitute a productive basis for the next step—personal evaluation meetings.

(2)   Pupil−teacher evaluation meeting
On the basis of children's answers to the above questions, the teacher holds personal meetings with those children who seem to be demonstrating under-achievement behaviour. During this meeting the teacher attempts to find out whether the child's interests, hobbies and behaviour at home shed further light on the child's school behaviour and possible discrepancies between the pupil's intellectual abilities and actual school performance.
(3)   Data collection
The teacher studies the school records of these children, and consults the head teacher and staff for further relevant information.

6. CONDUCTING THE COURSE

During subsequent course meetings the teachers are introduced to the characteristics, problems and behaviours of underachievers and to the principles of the intervention programme described in Chapter 5. Each meeting is first devoted to the study of one of the theoretical issues explaining underachievement, followed by a workshop in which teachers report and discuss their weekly work with their underachievers and receive guidance, reinforcement and support.

7. EVALUATION

At the end of the course participants evaluate both their own ability to understand and help underachieving pupils and the progress made by their underachievers, utilizing the following criteria:

(1)   Comparison between previous and present scholastic performance in different subjects.

(2) Comparison between previous and present participation in lessons and completion of assignments.
(3) Positive changes in behaviour.
(4) Improvement in school attendance.
(5) The child's personal evaluation of progress made.

(8) FOLLOW–UP

Finally, teachers are encouraged to widen the scope of the intervention treatment by including more underachieving pupils in the programme and to share the understanding and experience they have gained with other members of their school staff.

STUDENT–TEACHER EDUCATION: AN INTEGRATIVE APPROACH

The second model aims to provide student-teachers with the psychological and educational background needed for gaining an insight into the problems of underachievers in school. Since this model was based on the rationale and experience derived from a pilot programme stimulated by the Plowden recommendations (1967), and conducted at Goldsmiths' College, it should be helpful first to outline the principles and structure of this programme. Relevant to our discussion is the emphasis made by the Plowden Report on the need for creating closer links between schools of education and schools in order to foster educational progress at all levels of education. Subsequently, London University's Goldsmiths College hosted a committee, chaired by Lady Plowden, to examine the implications of the recommendations of the Plowden Report for Higher Education. As a member of this committee, I became interested in investigating the possibility of creating educationally meaningful links with the schools in which the college students did their teaching practice. It seemed to me that such links could be developed by creating shared learning experiences which would involve the active participation of students and teachers. With the cooperation of the LCC Inspector of Schools, Mr Hayling, the proposal was accepted by the schools and a group of deputy heads and senior teachers were selected for participation in this project.

The introductory course in educational psychology was chosen as an appropriate theoretical basis for the course curriculum activities which aimed at creating a significant learning-teaching situation which could be 'transferred' to the school situation. With the cooperation of the school inspector eight senior teachers were selected to participate with my group of students in a programme which consisted of the following merger of college and school activities:

(1) Lecture in Educational Psychology.
(2) Student-teacher group discussion, chaired by a practising teacher.
(3) College workshop—each term one curriculum area was selected for the purpose of creating appropriate materials and teaching methods, based on the

theoretical principle studied. Student-teachers worked together with their 'leader'—the school teacher. A college curriculum specialist joined us in this activity. For example, one term was devoted to the role of creativity in children's development and learning. While the theoretical issues were introduced by me, the curriculum art workshop was conducted by Mr Grater. The photographs in Figures 9.1 and 9.2 were taken during one of the workshops at Goldsmiths College.

(4) Field work. The following day was devoted to field work. Each group of students spent the morning in the school of 'their' teacher. Guided by the teacher, each student worked with a group of children implementing the teaching methods developed together in college.

(5) Feedback. At the beginning of subsequent weekly meetings in college, the participants discussed experiences and problems encountered in school. The shared educational experiences created significant links between the schools and the college, enhanced the relevance of college education for the students, increased the understanding of children's development and problems of both students and teachers and was instrumental in introducing appropriate and innovative teaching methods into schools.

While the approach outlined above can be utilized for the teaching of various curriculum areas, it is particularly appropriate for providing student-teachers with the theoretical background and educational experience required for understanding and later on coping with one of the most serious and complex problems prevailing in schools. The following model was designed by me for this purpose as part of the curriculum of the University of Haifa, School of Education.

THE NATURE AND TREATMENT OF UNDERACHIEVE-MENT: AN INTEGRATIVE COURSE FOR STUDENT–TEACHERS AND PRACTISING TEACHERS

1. PARTICIPANTS

(1) A university lecturer in Educational Psychology (in this case, myself).
(2) Thirty third-year student-teachers
(3) Six senior class teachers, teaching children of superior and average ability.

2. OBJECTIVES

(1) Creating a meaningful learning situation for the study of a relevant problem both for student-teachers and for practising teachers.
(2) Developing a deeper understanding of underachieving children of different abilities by means of the integration of theory and practice.
(3) Providing tools for the treatment of underachievement and the means to implement and evaluate them in school.

Figure 9.1 Creative workshop: Art tutor, practising teachers and student teachers at Goldsmiths College

Figure 9.2 Education lecturer and students during a combined course for initial and in-service training of teachers

(4) To initiate learning-teaching processes that can be developed with under-achievers in the classroom situation.

(5) To encourage practising teachers to participate in educational innovation developed in colleges of education for the purpose of improving the educational environment of underachievers.

(6) To increase the involvement of schools of education in the problems of the field, in general, and those of underachievers, in particular.

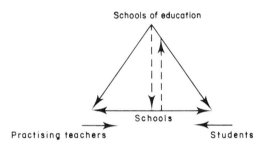

Figure 9.3   Integrating theory and practice in schools
of education

3. CURRICULUM

(a) Theoretical background

(1) The nature, origins, scope and identification of scholastic underachievement.
(2) Personality variables and characteristics of underachievers of different levels of ability.
(3) Influences of home, culture and society on underachievement.
(4) School factors.

(b) Educational practice

(1) Intervention programmes capable of alleviating behavioural and learning difficulties of underachievers.
(2) Structuring relevant education environment.
(3) Teaching methods conducive to reducing underachievement in school.

Sources

(1) Theoretical sources can be found in Chapters 1−3 and in the Bibliography.
(2) Intervention treatment and teaching methods are provided in Chapters 5−7.

4. PROCEDURE

(a) Course activities

Weekly meetings at the School of Education for all participants—student-teachers and practising teachers—were devoted to two activities.

(1) Lecture and discussion: 1 hour. The theoretical issues explaining under-achievement and their educational implications.

(2) Workshop: 1 hour. For this purpose each teacher worked with a group of students on the practical applications of the theoretical considerations raised in the lecture for the classroom situation in terms of the needs of underachieving children.

(b) School experiences

(i) Student practice

During the week each group of students visited 'their' teacher in school and worked with one underachieving pupil in class. Since all the children in the class were engaged in individual work, the teacher was able to provide help when necessary.

(ii) Teacher follow-up

Practising teachers participating in the course tried out the intervention programme with one or two of their underachievers.

(c) Feedback

Each subsequent course meeting began with participants reporting on their field experiences.

(d) Counselling

Guidance and counselling is provided by the course lecturer in schools. It also gives the lecturer an opportunity to see the students at work and to discuss the need for on-going intervention for underachievers with the head teacher and the school staff.

(e) Evaluation

At the end of the course, head teachers of the schools involved in the programme, the school counsellor and school psychologist join the course participants at the School of Education for a final session devoted to the evaluation of the course in terms of its contribution to the understanding of the problems of underachievers in school and its efficacy for the improvement of the educational environment and school performance of underachieving children.

5. CONCLUSIONS

In the light of the experience derived from the implementation of the models described above, it seems possible to conclude that the integration of theory and prac-tice served both to increase the motivation of the course participants to try out the ideas and methods which were introduced during the course and to deepen their involvement with their underachieving pupils. Furthermore, an important by-product of the course was the growing concern of the schools for the problems of their underachieving children. While it is not suggested that widespread changes in the school situation of underachievers can be achieved as a result of participation in one single course, it seems possible to assume that when such courses become an integral part of teacher education, they will constitute a continuing educational process capable of inducing greater motivation at all levels of education to assume responsibility for introducing the educational changes needed for alleviating the problems of underachievers and thus contributing to reducing the incidences of manifested underachievement in schools.

Studying Primary School Underachievers of Average and Superior Ability

APPENDIX A: EDUCATIONAL MEASURES

1. MEAN SCHOOL GRADE

For each pupil a mean grade was calculated from grades in all the school subjects taken during that year. Grades could range from 4 (fail) to 10 (excellent). Mean grades over all pupils were then calculated for each group in the experimental design.

2. GRADE WITH CLASS TEACHER

A mean grade for each research group was calculated over the grades which each pupil received from the class teacher.

3. TARDINESS

A mean group score was computed for the number of incidences of lateness recorded by the class teacher for each pupil. (Range for individual pupils: 0−30.)

4. ABSENCES

Mean group scores reflected the average recorded absences over all pupils in each group. (Range for individual pupils: 0−30.)

5,6,7. BEHAVIOUR IN CLASS, PARTICIPATION IN CLASS AND SOCIAL ACTIVITY

Non-academic aspects of behaviour in Israeli schools are rated on a scale ranging from 1 (very poor) to 7 (excellent) in standard report cards. Mean grades for each group were computed for overall behaviour, participation in class and social activity.

8/1. PUPILS' ATTITUDES

Pupils' attitudes towards their schools were derived from a questionnaire. For each question, pupils were required to rate their attitudes on a five-point scale where higher ratings indicated more positive attitudes as depicted below.

0	1	2	3	4
Not at all	Hardly at all	Somewhat	Very	Very much indeed

The ratings for all questions were summed so that a pupil's score could range from 0—20. Group means were then computed as described above.

8/2. ENGLISH TRANSLATION OF THE PUPILS' ATTITUDE QUESTIONNAIRE

Name_____ Class_____

Rate your answers on a five-point scale. Put the appropriate number of the scale next to each question.

0	1	2	3	4
Not at all	Hardly at all	Somewhat	Very	Very much indeed

(1) Do you like going to school?
(2) Is your school useful to you?
(3) Do you find your class and school interesting?
(4) Do you think that your school has good teachers?
(5) Do you think that your school is a good school?

APPENDIX B: PSYCHOLOGICAL MEASURES

1/1. SELF–CONCEPT

An Israeli adaptation (Ziv and Shechori, 1968) of Rogers' child adaptation test was used to provide a measure of self-concept. This measure was selected because it has been found suitable for use with Israeli samples. In addition, this measure seemed appropriate since it derives from a theoretical orientation to the individual very similar to that which guided the present study. The questionnaire consists of twenty-five items each of which describes a theoretical child and asks the subject to rate the degree of perceived similarity with herself. Ratings are on a scale of 1—5 as depicted below.

1	2	3	4	5
Not at all similar	Hardly similar	Quite similar	Very similar	Exactly the same

For analysis, the most negative rating was awarded 1/5 of a point and the most positive one point.

Responses on all items were summed yielding a minimum score of 2.5 and a maximum score of 25 over all items for each pupil. Group means were then computed in the usual fashion.

1/2. ENGLISH TRANSLATION OF THE SELF–CONCEPT QUESTIONNAIRE

Name_____ Class_____

The following short descriptions describe various children. Please rate each description on a scale of 1–5 as to your similarity with each described child. Put the appropriate number of the scale next to each question.

1	2	3	4	5
Not at all similar	Hardly similar	Quite similar	Very similar	Exactly the same

(1) Tamar (Ehud) is the most gifted pupil in our class.
(2) Ruth (Ben) is a very friendly child.
(3) Shula (Giora) is always jolly.
(4) Lea (Dudu) is not an active child.
(5) Rachel (Abraham) is a very shy child.
(6) Nurit (David) is very obedient at home.
(7) Ada (Reuben) has a strong will.
(8) Rina (Chaim) is always the leader of her (his) friends.
(9) Galit (Moses) is very jealous of her (his) brothers and sisters.
(10) Galila (Meir) does not listen to her (his) parents as she (he) thinks she (he) knows everything better than everybody.
(11) Chana (Jacob) prefers dreaming to doing things.
(12) Dorit (Israel) always quarrels with her (his) brothers and sisters.
(13) Dalia (Shimon) is an independent child who likes to make her/his own decisions.
(14) Esther (Aron) makes friends easily.
(15) Osnat (Michael) is very talented.
(16) Ofra (ofer) is always willing to help at home.
(17) Shula (Joshua) is very tidy.
(18) Rachel (Yoav) always seeks attention.
(19) Tova (Zevi) likes school.
(20) Yona (Jonathan) is a very quiet child.
(21) Ronit (Raphael) gets excited about everything.
(22) Efrat (Ephraim) gets angry easily.

144

(23) Edna (Uzi) is very impatient.
(24) Sharon (Yochanan) is a very good pupil.
(25) Chava (Raphael) understands everything in class.

2/1. LOCUS OF CONTROL

Locus of control was measured using the Tel Aviv Locus of Control Test constructed by Milgram *et al.* (1974) as an integration of the approaches of Rotter (1966) and Crandall *et al.* (1965).

The test consists of 30 items each of which offers two alternative reasons, one 'internal' and the other 'external', for a hypothetical behaviour. The items cover different situations at home and at school.

The advantages of this test for the puposes of this study are:

(1) It relates to spheres covering most of the sources argued here to be relevant to the phenomenon of underachievement (see Chapter 2).
(2) The test allows for the choice of one of several alternative responses to each item and thus provides a more sensitive and differentiated measure of locus of control than many other instruments.
(3) The test was specially developed for use with an Israeli population.

For each item the child is requested to choose one of five alternatives on a five-point scale where higher scores reflect greater internal control,

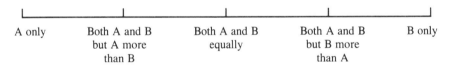

| A only | Both A and B but A more than B | Both A and B equally | Both A and B but B more than A | B only |

where A and B are the external and internal alternatives respectively. The most internal alternative was awarded one point and the least one-fifth of a point. Responses over all items were summed yielding possible minimum score of 6 and a maximum score of 30 for each pupil. Group means were then computed.

2/2. ENGLISH TRANSLATION OF THE LOCUS OF CONTROL TEST

Name_____ Class_____

We are interested to know what children of your age think and feel about different matters. This questionnaire does not test knowledge or school achievements, and does not consist of right or wrong answers. We would like you to answer sincerely so that we could obtain a true general picture.

Directions

This questionnaire includes sentences, each describing a certain situation. Perhaps the sentence describes a situation which has never happened to you. In this case try to imagine how you would feel and behave in such a situation.

Two possible explanations follow each sentence. You may feel that either possibility 'A' or possibility 'B' describe your feelings. On the other hand, you may think that both 'A' and 'B' describe the causes of the situation; in this case you must decide which of the two is more relevant.

We shall now demonstrate how you should answer this questionnaire. Mark an 'X' over the correct answer.

(1)   When you solve problems in mathematics easily, it it generally because:
(a)   You studied a lot before you began to solve these problems?
(b)   The teacher gave easy problems?

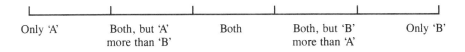

| Only 'A' | Both, but 'A' more than 'B' | Both | Both, but 'B' more than 'A' | Only 'B' |

(2)   Most of the sad events are a result of:
(a)   Bad luck,
(b)   One's own mistakes.
(3)   When your parents praise you, it is because:
(a)   They are in a good mood.
(b)   You did something to justify praise.
(4)   Your teacher praised your behaviour. It is because:
(a)   Your behaviour was excellent.
(b)   Your teacher was in a good mood.
(5)   When you quarrel with your friends, is it because:
(a)   Your friends generally pick a quarrel with you?
(b)   You are not prepared to compromise?
(6)   When you fight with other children, is it because:
(a)   You generally do not consider the wishes of others?
(b)   Children always pick on you?
(7)   When your teacher tells you to 'improve your school performance', it is because:
(a)   Teachers always say so in order to make the pupils try harder.
(b)   Your achievements were lower than usual.
(8)   When the teacher gives you a high grade in a test, is it because:
(a)   You had good luck?
(b)   You were well prepared for the test?
(9)   Let us say that you moved to a new place and that you did not succeed in making new friends. It happened because:
(a)   You have not made sufficient efforts to make new friends.
(b)   It is a close social situation and the children are not interested in new friends.

(10) When your brother or sister is angry with you, is it because:
(a) You have annoyed him/her?
(b) He/she is just angry with you?
(11) Success in life is more:
(a) A matter of luck?
(b) A result of invested efforts?
(12) You went with your family for a holiday. During the holiday you met new friends who asked you to play with them. It is because:
(a) You were friendly and pleasant to them?
(b) They were friendly children who usually ask other children to play with them?
(13) Unfortunate events happen as a result of:
(a) Mistakes?
(b) Events that cannot be controlled?
(14) When you best friends treat you well, is it because:
(a) They are nice to you?
(b) You are a good friend and thus it is only fair that they treat you well?
(15) Let us imagine that your parents say that you are not studying enough for school and they forbid you to go out to play. It happened because:
(a) They have exaggerated demands.
(b) You really did not study enough.
(16) When a person has good traits, is it because:
(a) He/she inherited these traits?
(b) His/Her experiences shaped them?
(17) Your friends removed you from the game. Is it because:
(a) You did not play well?
(b) Despite the fact that you played well, it is good to give another child a chance to play.
(18) When you forget something that was said in class, it is probably because:
(a) The teacher did not explain well.
(b) You did not make an effort to remember.
(19) You were elected to the class committee. It is because:
(a) You had succeeded in similar duties.
(b) Your friends like you.
(20) Let us imagine that you moved to a new neighbourhood. You made new friends and became their leader. Is it because:
(a) You have the right traits to become a leader?
(b) You joined a group that can easily be led?
(21) When the teacher reproaches you in class, is it because:
(a) The teacher simply picked on you as it was noisy in the class?
(b) You talked to your neighbour and disturbed the teacher?
(22) When you quarrel with your parents
(a) It is usually your fault.
(b) It is generally their fault.
(23) When someone has become a leader, is it because:

(a) He/she made good use of the opportunities that occurred?
(b) Luck helped him/her?
(24) Success is a matter of:
(a) The right opportunity.
(b) Hard work.
(25) Let us imagine that you and your sister or brother received a book as a present. You both want to read the book first. After a long argument you win. Is it because:
(a) Your parents intervened in your favour?
(b) You managed to convince your sister or brother that you should be the first to read the book?
(26) When you offend your brother or sister, is it because:
(a) You usually get cross when things are not going smoothly for you?
(b) They oppose you in an offensive manner?
(27) When you succeed in a subject that is difficult for you, is it because:
(a) You were lucky that someone helped you?
(b) You tried harder than usual?
(28) When a plan fails to materialize, is it because:
(a) People did not plan well?
(b) Many things are, anyhow, the result of fate?
(29) When you have difficulties in solving the problems in mathematics given in class, is it generally because:
(a) You did not study enough?
(b) The teacher gave particularly difficult problems?
(30) When you compete with your brother and sister and win, is it because:
(a) You are better than them in this game?
(b) You were lucky?

3. NEED ACHIEVEMENT AND NEED AFFILIATION

Need achievement and need affiliation were measured employing the 'Test of Human Insight', constructed by French (1958) as an adaptation of McClelland *et al's* measure of need achievement (1953). This measure was selected as appropriate for the purpose of this study for the following reasons:

(1) The test was found by Shaw (1961) to differentiate effectively between achievers and underachievers.
(2) The test consists of verbal cues instead of the pictorial ones used by McClelland which makes it most suitable for use with children as it eliminates such extraneous factors as age and appearances. In addition, it is possible to test boys and girls at the same time, by changing only the name of the child in the verbal cues.
(3) It was shown in Chapter 2 that studying the interactive effects of need achievement and need affiliation has been productive in the research of underachievement. The measure consists of ten written cues, each of which

describes a theoretical situation and asks the subject to write a few sentences about the person described in the cue—what he is like, what she wants, what will happen to him in the future and their opinion of this person. Responses to the cues were scored for need achievement and need affiliation imagery separately, according to the seven criteria set by French. Each subcategory was only scored once, so that the individual's need achievement and need affiliation scores could each range from a minimum of 0 to a maximum of 7. Group means were then computed.

4. FEAR OF FAILURE

Fear of failure was measured using the French 'Test of Human Insight' described above. The rationale for selecting a measure of need achievement for the purpose of tapping Fear of Failure was derived from the theories of McClelland (1953) and Atkinson (1958) who found that responses to TAT cues designed to measure need achievement could be successfully employed to isolate the motive of Fear of Failure (see Chapter 2).

This measure seemed appropriate for the purpose of this study since it derives from a theoretical orientation to motivation very similar to that which guided the present study (see Chapter 2).

Moulton's (1958) method of scoring was utilized. Accordingly, responses to the written cues were coded for Fear of Failure when they evidence Fear of Failure imagery as defined by the seven categories established by Moulton (1958).

Each category was scored only once, although it may have appeared more than once in the same response. The individual's Fear of Failure score consisted of the total sum of categories noted and thus could range from a minimum of 0 to a maximum of 7. Group means were then computed.

English Translation of the Test of Human Insight
This questionnaire examines the reasons for children's behaviour. The following statements describe someone's typical behaviour which you are asked to explain. Read each description and then decide what is the reason for this behaviour, what kind of a child he/she is, what are his/her wishes and what are the results of his/her behaviour. If you think of more that one reason, select the most likely one.
Write your answers after each statement.

(1)   Jacob (Yael) prefers following others, rather than leading them.
(2)   Dan (Dina) always tries something new.
(3)   Yigal (Gila) said: 'I am sure that I can do it'.
(4)   Shimon (Sara) is worried about his/her success in the coming examinations.
(5)   Roni (Ronit) invests much more effort in studying than other children.
(6)   It is very important to Yossi (Rina) what his/her friends think of him/her.
(7)   Uri (Orah) is always prepared to help his/her friends.
(8)   David (Dvora) is sad when someone blames him/her.
(9)   Michael (Michal) said 'They will not ask me to join them'.

(10)   Arie (Ariela) said: 'Look what I have done'.

Scoring categories for the Test of Insight (developed by French, 1958)

(1)   Desire for goal.
(2)   Goal-directed activity.
(3)   Personal qualifications for goal attainment.
(4)   Expectation of goal attainment.
(5)   Goal attainment.
(6)   Positive affect to goal attainment.
(7)   Defensive statements or rationalization.

Scoring categories for Fear of Failure (developed by Moulton 1958).

(1)   Fear of failure imagery.
(2)   A desire to leave a situation in which achievement evaluation might take place.
(3)   Any indication of activity which is not or has not been going smoothly.
(4)   Anticipation of failure.
(5)   Hostile press (criticism or prediction of failure)
(6)   Personal obstacles and environmental obstacles.
(7)   Fear thema.

5. FEAR OF SUCCESS

An Israeli adaptation (Butler and Nisan, 1975) of Horner's (1968) measure of avoidance of success was used to provide a measure of Fear of Success. The measure was selected because it has been found suitable for use with Israeli samples. In addition, this measure seemed appropriate since it derives from a theoretical orientation similar to that which guided the present study (see Chapter 2).

The questionnaire consisted of three verbal leads based on Horner's (1968) cues. As in Horner's (1968) study, girls received leads with names of girls and boys with names of boys. Subjects were asked to describe the person in the lead, what he/she wants, what he/she likes, what will happen to the person in the future and what they thought of this person.

Responses to the questionnaire were scored for Fear of Success imagery according to the seven categories defined by Horner (1968) and based on McClelland's (1953) Original Criteria (see Chapter 2). Every category was scored once only, so that a subjects' Fear of Success score could range from a minimum of 0 to a maximum of 7. Group means were then computed as described above.

English Translation of the Fear of Success Test
The following statements describe different situations. Read each statement and describe the subsequent thoughts and feelings of each child in each described event. Write your answers in the spaces which follow each statement.

(1)   When the examinations finished, Shoshana (Shimshon) discovered that she (he) had obtained the highest grades.
(2)   Ilana (Ilan) was awarded the first prize in the national competition in mathematics.
(3)   Rina (Ron), who is a brilliant pupil, is moving to a new school. She/he says to her/himself: 'I hope that the pupils in the new school will accept me'.

Scoring categories: (Horner, 1968)

(1)   Negative consequences because of success.
(2)   Anticipation of negative consequences.
(3)   Negative affect because of success.
(4)   Instrumental activity away from present or future success (i.e. learning female occupations).
(5)   Expression of conflict about success.
(6)   Denial of the situation described by cue.
(7)   Bizarre or inappropriate responses to the situation described by the cue.

APPENDIX C: TREATMENT MEASURES

English Translation of the Treatment Contract

A contract to be signed between:

The pupil _____

The teacher _____

for the duration of three months:

Commencing date _____ Terminating date _____

I, the teacher_____

undertake to award the following rewards for
each task:

Reward 1:
        2:
        3:

I, the pupil_____

undertake to accomplish the following tasks:

Task 1:
    2:
    3:

The evaluation of the accomplishment of tasks and the award of rewards will be conducted each week during a special weekly session.

The contract will be completed weekly. The weekly session will take place on:

Day _____

Hour _____

In the case that one of the sides feels that the other side is not fulfilling the contract's terms, he/she should ask for a special emergency meeting to be arranged, in order to discuss this matter.

Signed:

The pupil_____ The teacher_____

APPENDIX D: TEACHER MEASURES

Teacher attitudes were ascertained by means of a questionnaire. Responses to each item made up a four-point scale where higher scores reflected greater recognition of the need for change, higher expectations from the pupil and treatment and greater acceptance of personal responsibility. For each teacher an average score for each pupil was calculated over all five questions. When teachers answered for more than one pupil, average scores within each area were summed up and then divided by the number of pupils.

The English Translation of the Teacher Attitudes Questionnaire

Pupil's name _____ Teacher's name _____

Directions: Your response will help us to get to know your underachieving pupil. Please respond to the appropriate answer with an 'X' above the line (e.g. 1(X), 2(X), 3(X), 4(X) next to each question.

(1)   It seems to me that the problems of this pupil are temporary and that he/she will be able to solve them soon.

I agree	I agree	I do not	I definitely
completely		agree	do not agree

(2)   The pupil tries to improve but is unable to do so.

(3)   If the treatment had begun sometime ago, the pupil's school difficulties might have already disappeared.

(4)   The help that I could give this pupil should contribute to his/her progress in school.

(5)   The weekly sessions are pleasant; however, fewer sessions would be just as useful.

(6)   I believe that I could help this pupil improve his/her scholastic performance.

(7)   Would you have chosen this pupil for treatment?

(8)   Even if a great deal of effort should be invested in helping this pupil, he/she would not improve his/her achievements.

(9)   If this pupil would cooperate, it would be possible to improve his/her school situation.

(10)   This pupil has superior ability, if I could provide him/her with appropriate help, he/she would succeed in school.

(11)   This pupil might succeed in his/her studies if the factors that disturb him/her should disappear.

(12)   I would have preferred to limit my help to this pupil to the normal classroom situation.

(13)   This pupil could only progress significantly if I could help him/her personally.

(14)   This pupil could reach a much higher level of attainments.

(15)   The group sessions help me to conduct the treatment with this child.

(16)   Prolonged psychological help would be more useful in helping this child.

(17)   Systematic effort on behalf of this pupil would result in an improvement in his/her school achievements.

(18)   The group sessions contribute towards gaining a deeper insight into this child's problems.

(19)   The improvement of this pupil depends on the amount of the effort that I could invest in helping him/her.

(20)   This pupil functions in school accordingly to his/her ability.

APPENDIX E: METHODOLOGY AND OUTCOMES

1. CHILD VARIABLES

This study's first set of questions was concerned with the characteristics of the academic underachievers on a wide range of educational and psychological variables associated with underachievement. In addition, this study was interested in comparing the characteristics of underachievers of average and superior ability. Finally, the relationship between these characteristics and the intervention was examined.

Prior to investigation of the relationship between the characteristics of the underachievers and the intervention, the overall picture of the educational and psychological variables of the entire research population, before and after the treatment, was ascertained.

Since the aim in this case was to compare statistically the mean of the six research groups included in the study, a one-way analysis of variance was performed for each variable, on pre- and post intervention scores respectively and on the change scores. No *a priori* hypotheses as to group differences in the variables under study prior to intervention were formulated, as the aims of these comparisons were both exploratory, and to provide relevant information to the teachers participating in the intervention treatment. While it was hypothesized that the intervention would have a positive effect on the various educational variables under study, questions as to the effects of the intervention on the psychological variables were left open, since it was not clear that a short-term intervention would affect underlying psychological dispositions.

2. EDUCATIONAL VARIABLES

(a) Mean school grade

The results of the one-way analyses of variance for this variable are presented in Table 1. As might be expected, before treatment the mean school grades among both experimental and control gifted groups were higher than those among average-ability groups. After intervention, the significant group effect was due to the tendency of experimental groups of both ability levels to achieve higher grades than the control groups.

(b) Mean school grade with treatment teacher

The results of this variable, presented in Table 2, indicate a significant group effect for scores both before and after intervention and for the change scores.

(c) Tardiness

Somewhat surprisingly, the findings for tardiness indicate a significant group effect *prior* to intervention, with experimental groups of both ability levels tending to be late more often than the control groups. This trend is reversed after intervention, when the significant group effect derives from the fact that the control groups were now late more often than the experimental ones. Analysis of change scores reveals significant group effect derived from the fact that pupils in the experimental groups greatly reduced their tardiness—far more than did those in the control groups. In fact, tardiness in two of the control groups (GRC and AAG) even tended to *increase* over the duration of the study (see Table 3).

(d) Absences

The results for this variable, presented as Table 4, are very similar to those reported for tardiness. Again there is a significant group effect both before and after intervention, the former deriving from the tendency of experimental pupils to be absent more often than control ones, a tend reversed after intervention.

Table 1. Comparison of the change in mean scores of mean school grade by groups

Mean school grade	Before			After			Change		
Group	Mean	S.D.	N	Mean	S.D.	N	Mean	S.D.	N
1. GSC ⎤	5.75	0.62	12	7.58	0.90	12	1.83	0.72	12
2. GRC ⎬ Experimental	5.58	0.51	12	7.92	0.99	12	2.33	0.78	12
3. AAG ⎦	4.75	0.45	12	6.67	0.65	12	1.92	0.79	12
4. GSC ⎤	6.00	0.00	12	6.25	0.45	12	0.25	0.45	12
5. GRC ⎬ Control	5.92	0.29	12	6.17	0.39	12	0.25	0.45	12
6. AAG ⎦	5.17	0.39	12	5.50	0.52	12	0.33	0.49	12
For entire population	5.53	0.60	72	6.68	1.07	72	1.15	1.08	72
* One-way analysis of variance	*F = 15.34 df = 5 p = 0.000			*F = 21.07 df = 5 p = 0.000			*F = 28.43 df = 5 p = 0.000		

Table 2. Comparison of before, after and the change in mean scores of school grade with treatment teacher by groups

School grade and treatment teacher	Before			After			Change		
Group	Mean	S.D.	N	Mean	S.D.	N	Mean	S.D.	N
1. GSC ⎤	5.75	0.62	12	7.67	0.98	12	1.92	0.67	12
2. GRC ⎬ Experimental	5.58	0.51	12	8.03	1.08	12	2.50	0.80	12
3. AAG ⎦	4.92	0.29	12	6.67	0.65	12	1.75	0.62	12
4. GSC ⎤	6.00	0.00	12	6.42	0.51	12	0.42	0.51	12
5. GRC ⎬ Control	6.00	0.43	12	6.67	0.49	12	0.67	0.49	12
6. AAG ⎦	5.17	0.39	12	5.33	0.49	12	0.17	0.39	12
For entire population	5.57	0.58	72	6.81	1.15	72	1.24	1.04	72
* One-way analysis of variance	*F = 13.37 df = 5			*F = 20.53 df = 5			*F = 30.19 df = 5		

Table 3. Comparison of before, after and the change in mean scores of tardiness by groups

Tardiness Group	Before Mean	Before S.D.	Before N	After Mean	After S.D.	After N	Change Mean	Change S.D.	Change N
1. GSC ⎤	5.17	1.75	12	2.55	1.04	12	-2.82	1.17	12
2. GRC ⎥ — Experimental	6.83	1.64	12	2.33	0.89	12	-4.50	1.88	12
3. AAG ⎦	6.08	0.90	12	2.00	0.85	12	-4.08	1.44	12
4. GSC ⎤	4.45	1.57	12	3.45	0.37	12	-1.10	0.57	12
5. GRC ⎥ — Control	4.92	1.38	12	6.08	1.62	12	1.17	0.58	12
6. AAG ⎦	4.00	0.60	12	5.17	0.94	12	1.17	0.72	12
For entire population	5.25	1.64	72	3.61	1.91	72	-1.70	2.61	72
* One-way analysis of variance	*F = 6.99 df = 5 p = 0.000			*F = 25.07 df = 5 p = 0.000			*F = 54.08 df = 5 p = 0.000		

Table 4. Comparison of before, after and the change in mean scores of absences by groups

Absence Group	Before Mean	Before S.D.	Before N	After Mean	After S.D.	After N	Change Mean	Change S.D.	Change N
1. GSC ⎤	7.33	1.77	12	2.58	1.08	12	-4.75	1.29	12
2. GRC ⎥ — Experimental	6.58	1.50	12	2.33	1.00	12	-4.67	1.73	12
3. AAG ⎦	6.83	1.27	12	2.17	1.27	12	-4.67	1.97	12
4. GSC ⎤	5.58	1.16	12	5.08	1.16	12	-0.50	1.00	12
5. GRC ⎥ — Control	5.75	1.29	12	7.17	1.11	12	1.42	1.08	12
6. AAG ⎦	5.42	1.31	12	7.33	1.30	12	1.92	0.67	12
For entire population	6.25	1.40	72	4.54	2.49	72	-1.75	3.21	72
* One-way analysis of variance	*F = 3.69 df = 5 p = 0.005			*F = 49.52 df = 5 p = 0.000			*F = 65.03 df = 5 p = 0.000		

(e) Behaviour in class

As Table 5 reveals, a significant effect for group in all three analyses was found. Before treatment this derives mainly from the relatively poor ratings awarded two of the experimental groups (GRC and AAG). After treatment the ratings of the experimental groups were generally higher than those of the controls, with the exception of the gifted in special classes who surprisingly rated highest of all groups. The extremely high standard deviation suggests that this increase probably derived from marked behavioural improvement in a few of the twelve subjects.

(f) Participation in class

Findings for this variable, presented in Table 6, again reveal a significant group effect. After treatment the main difference was between experimental and control groups, with the former scoring far higher on participation.

(g) Social activity

The picture for this variable both before and after treatment, presented in Table 7, is very similar to that received for behaviour and participation, confirming the favourable effects of the intervention.

(h) Pupils' attitudes

The result of this variable are presented as Table 8. Again, the results of all three analyses reveal a significant effect for group. While prior to treatment this derived simply from scatter among group means, after treatment it derived from the more favourable attitudes of experimental as compared with control subjects and from the positive change in attitudes found among experimental but not control groups.

To conclude, the findings confirmed the hypothesis that the intervention would have a favourable effect on various aspects of educational functioning. While the results also showed that the initial status of the various groups on the educational variables differed, these differences did not derive from any consistent differences between gifted and average-ability groups.

3. PSYCHOLOGICAL VARIABLES

Since these variables tap underlying psychological characteristics formed and maintained over a long period, no general hypotheses as to the effects of these variables were formulated, as it was not considered reasonable to expect marked changes after twelve treatment sessions. The variables were included in the study for the information they could provide as to the initial characteristics of the underachievers studied, possible differences between gifted and average ability underachievers, and to investigate whether any of the characteristics were affected by the intervention. Thus the analyses for these variables were identical to those described above for the educational variables.

Table 5. Comparison of before, after and the change in mean scores of evaluation of behaviour by groups

Evaluation of behaviour	Before			After			Change		
Group	Mean	S.D.	N	Mean	S.D.	N	Mean	S.D.	N
1. GSC ⎤	3.67	1.56	12	5.92	1.31	12	2.25	0.87	12
2. GRC ⎥ — Experimental	2.83	0.94	12	5.75	1.22	12	2.92	1.24	12
3. AAG ⎦	2.25	0.45	12	5.33	0.98	12	3.08	0.90	12
4. GSC ⎤	3.50	0.67	12	6.42	4.62	12	2.92	4.52	12
5. GRC ⎥ — Control	3.67	0.65	12	4.17	0.94	12	0.50	0.67	12
6. AAG ⎦	3.67	0.49	12	3.17	0.83	12	-0.50	0.67	12
For entire population	3.26	1.01	72	5.12	2.34	72	1.86	2.39	72
* One-way analysis of variance	$*F = 5.46$ $df = 5$ $p = 0.000$			$*F = 3.98$ $df = 5$ $p = 0.003$			$*F = 6.65$ $df = 5$ $p = 0.000$		

Table 6. Comparison of before, after and the change in mean scores of participation in class by groups

Class participation	Before			After			Change		
Group	Mean	S.D.	N	Mean	S.D.	N	Mean	S.D.	N
1. GSC ⎤	2.08	0.51	12	5.17	0.94	12	3.08	1.00	12
2. GRC ⎥ — Experimental	1.92	0.51	12	5.08	1.16	12	3.17	0.94	12
3. AAG ⎦	1.00	0.00	12	4.00	0.85	12	3.00	0.85	12
4. GSC ⎤	2.17	0.58	12	2.50	0.52	12	0.33	0.89	12
5. GRC ⎥ — Control	2.33	0.49	12	2.50	0.52	12	0.17	0.72	12
6. AAG ⎦	2.08	0.29	12	2.00	0.43	12	-0.08	0.29	12
For entire population	1.93	0.61	72	3.54	1.49	72	1.61	1.68	72
* One-way analysis of variance	$*F = 13.69$ $df = 5$ $p = 0.000$			$*F = 38.15$ $df = 5$ $p = 0.000$			$*F = 47.36$ $df = 5$ $p = 0.000$		

158

Table 7. Comparison of before, after and the change in mean scores of social activity by groups

Social activity Group	Before Mean	S.D.	N	After Mean	S.D.	N	Change Mean	S.D.	N
1. GSC ⎤	2.08	0.51	12	4.50	0.90	12	2.42	0.67	12
2. GRC — Experimental	1.83	0.39	12	4.75	1.22	12	2.92	1.44	12
3. AAG ⎦	1.08	0.29	12	4.25	0.96	12	3.17	1.11	12
4. GSC ⎤	2.00	0.00	12	2.33	0.49	12	0.33	0.49	12
5. GRC — Control	2.00	0.00	12	2.25	0.45	12	0.25	0.45	12
6. AAG ⎦	2.08	0.29	12	2.25	0.45	12	0.17	0.58	12
For entire population	1.85	0.46	72	3.39	1.37	72	1.54	1.56	72
* One-way analysis of variance	*F = 18.31 df = 5 p = 0.000			*F = 27.98 df = 5 p = 0.000			*F = 32.63 df = 5 p = 0.000		

Table 8. Comparison of before, after and the change in mean scores of pupils' attitude by groups

Attitude towards school Group	Before Mean	S.D.	N	After Mean	S.D.	N	Change Mean	S.D.	N
1. GSC ⎤	7.67	2.50	12	14.75	2.38	12	7.08	2.91	12
2. GRC — Experimental	6.17	3.35	12	14.25	3.67	12	8.08	3.48	12
3. AAG ⎦	3.17	1.03	12	12.83	3.66	12	9.67	4.33	12
4. GSC ⎤	5.00	2.66	12	6.08	3.09	12	1.08	0.79	12
5. GRC — Control	7.42	3.03	12	7.58	3.48	12	0.17	1.59	12
6. AAG ⎦	6.67	1.97	12	4.67	1.77	12	-2.00	0.85	12
For entire population	6.01	2.90	72	10.03	5.05	72	4.01	5.15	72
* One-way analysis of variance	*F = 5.32 df = 5 p = 0.000			*F = 24.68 df = 5 p = 0.000			*F = 39.17 df = 5 p = 0.000		

(a) Self-concept

While the results of the analyses of variance for this variable, presented in Table 9, indicate a significant effect for group prior to intervention, this was not due to a clear-cut difference between gifted and average ability groups. After intervention, the effect for group was not significant, but there was a significant group effect for the magnitude of change scores, derived primarily from the large positive changes in self-concept scores achieved by the two experimental groups, GRC and AAG.

(c) Locus of control

The findings for this variable, presented in Table 10, reveal that although there was no significant effect for group prior to intervention, the two groups of gifted pupils in special classes had the most internal scores while the two groups with the most external locus of control were the experimental GRC and AAG. The effect for group was significant after intervention and for the change scores. It is worth noting that all groups received more internal scores at the second testing except for the control average-ability group whose scores at second testing were more external.

(c) Need achievement

As shown in Table 11, the results indicated a significant effect for group both before and after treatment, although there was no effect for group on the change scores. Prior to intervention the differences in group means derived mainly from the relatively high scores on need achievement of the two groups of gifted pupils in regular classes. After treatment the group means followed a similar order, although the increase in the measured need achievement of the experimental groups GSC and AAG and the slight decrease in that of the control AAG are worth noting.

(d) Need affiliation

It is interesting that prior to intervention the highest scores were again achieved by the two groups of gifted children in regular classes. As revealed in Table 12, the picture changed after intervention, the change scores reflecting a generally more positive trend among the experimental groups.

(e) Fear of failure

The results for this variable, presented in Table 13, did not reveal a significant effect for group before intervention but after intervention the group effect was significant, with the three control groups scoring higher on fear of failure than the experimental ones.

(f) Fear of success

The findings for this variable reveal a significant effect for group; both before and after treatment, these gifted groups scored higher on fear of success than did the two

Table 9. Comparison of before, after and the change in mean scores of self-concept by groups

Self-concept Group	Before Mean	Before S.D.	N	After Mean	After S.D.	N	Change Mean	Change S.D.	N
1. GSC — Experimental	16.50	3.85	12	16.17	4.91	12	−0.33	3.60	12
2. GRC	10.25	4.83	12	14.25	4.25	12	4.00	3.86	12
3. AAG	7.08	4.14	12	11.42	3.68	12	4.33	2.99	12
4. GSC — Control	12.92	5.45	12	14.17	4.91	12	1.25	2.38	12
5. GRC	14.00	6.25	12	14.42	5.47	12	0.42	2.71	12
6. AAG	12.58	6.37	12	12.67	7.38	12	0.08	2.64	12
For entire population	12.22	5.86	72	13.85	5.30	72	1.62	3.51	72
* One-way analysis of variance	$*F = 4.58$ df = 5 p = 0.001			$*F = 1.15$ df = 5 p = 0.345			$*F = 5.26$ df = 5 p = 0.000		

Table 10. Comparison of before, after and the change in mean scores of locus of control by groups

Locus of control Group	Before Mean	Before S.D.	N	After Mean	After S.D.	N	Change Mean	Change S.D.	N
1. GSC — Experimental	17.50	7.81	12	20.17	6.93	12	2.67	4.58	12
2. GRC	14.92	5.36	12	19.42	4.89	12	4.50	4.68	12
3. AAG	13.92	6.36	12	19.08	5.99	12	5.17	4.88	12
4. GSC — Control	18.83	5.57	12	21.00	4.94	12	2.17	4.57	12
5. GRC	15.75	5.89	12	17.42	6.36	12	1.67	3.68	12
6. AAG	15.67	4.07	12	13.50	5.42	12	−1.55	4.48	12
For entire population	16.10	6.12	72	18.43	6.27	72	2.49	4.83	72
* One-way analysis of variance	$*F = 1.02$ df = 5 p = 0.412			$*F = 2.45$ df = 5 p = 0.043			$*F = 3.20$ df = 5 p = 0.012		

Table 11. Comparison of before, after and the change in mean scores of need achievement by groups

Need achievement Group	Before Mean	S.D.	N	After Mean	S.D.	N	Change Mean	S.D.	N
1. GSC ⎫	2.33	0.98	12	3.75	1.29	12	1.42	1.24	12
2. GRC ⎬ — Experimental	4.50	1.68	12	4.83	1.70	12	0.33	0.89	12
3. AAG ⎭	3.75	1.86	12	4.42	1.38	12	0.67	1.37	12
4. GSC ⎫	2.75	1.36	12	3.08	1.50	12	0.33	0.98	12
5. GRC ⎬ — Control	4.25	1.86	12	4.42	1.50	12	0.17	1.53	12
6. AAG ⎭	2.25	1.21	12	1.92	1.44	12	-0.33	0.98	12
For entire population	3.31	1.73	72	3.74	1.74	72	0.43	1.26	72
* One-way analysis of variance	$*F = 5.00$ df = 5 p = 0.000			$*F = 6.47$ df = 5 p = 0.000			$*F = 2.89$ df = 5 p = 0.20		

Table 12. Comparison of before, after and the change in mean scores of need affiliation by groups

Need affiliation Group	Before Mean	S.D.	N	After Mean	S.D.	N	Change Mean	S.D.	N
1. GSC ⎫	2.42	1.56	12	2.92	2.19	12	0.50	1.51	12
2. GRC ⎬ — Experimental	3.60	2.17	12	3.55	2.30	12	0.20	0.63	12
3. AAG ⎭	2.50	1.78	12	3.08	1.73	12	0.58	0.67	12
4. GSC ⎫	1.50	1.45	12	1.83	1.19	12	0.33	0.89	12
5. GRC ⎬ — Control	3.58	1.56	12	2.83	1.80	12	-0.75	1.05	12
6. AAG ⎭	1.42	0.79	12	1.42	0.51	12	0.00	0.85	12
For entire population	2.47	1.76	72	2.59	1.82	72	0.14	1.05	72
* One-way analysis of variance	$*F = 4.15$ df = 5 p = 0.002			$*F = 2.58$ df = 5 p = 0.034			$*F = 2.90$ df = 5 p = 0.020		

Table 13. Comparison of before, after and the change in mean scores of fear of failure by groups

Fear of failure		Before			After			Change		
Group		Mean	S.D.	N	Mean	S.D.	N	Mean	S.D.	N
1. GSC	Experimental	5.16	1.47	12	3.58	1.31	12	−1.58	1.24	12
2. GRC		4.33	1.56	12	3.17	0.94	12	−1.17	1.19	12
3. AAG		3.92	1.38	12	3.33	0.89	12	−0.58	1.31	12
4. GSC	Control	4.33	1.56	12	4.58	1.73	12	0.25	0.75	12
5. GRC		5.00	1.54	12	5.08	1.50	12	0.08	0.51	12
6. AAG		4.42	1.50	12	5.00	1.28	12	0.58	0.67	12
For entire population		4.53	1.51	72	4.12	1.49	72	−0.40	1.24	72
* One-way analysis of variance		$*F = 1.16$ df = 5 p = 0.336			$*F = 5.23$ df = 5 p = 0.000			$*F = 8.80$ df = 5 p = 0.000		

Table 14. Comparison of before, after and the change in mean scores of fear of success by groups

Fear of success		Before			After			Change		
Group		Mean	S.D.	N	Mean	S.D.	N	Mean	S.D.	N
1. GSC	Experimental	4.83	1.53	12	4.17	1.11	12	−0.66	0.78	12
2. GRC		3.92	1.38	12	3.58	0.90	12	−0.33	0.89	12
3. AAG		2.58	1.44	12	2.58	1.16	12	0.00	0.43	12
4. GSC	Control	3.25	1.71	12	3.50	1.62	12	0.25	0.45	12
5. GRC		4.17	2.04	12	4.42	2.06	12	0.25	0.62	12
6. AAG		2.00	0.43	12	2.50	0.52	12	0.50	0.52	12
For entire population		3.46	1.74	72	3.46	1.74	72	0.00	0.73	72
* One-way analysis of variance		$*F = 5.87$ df = 5			$*F = 4.24$ df = 5			$*F = 5.49$ df = 5		

average-ability groups. Interestingly, the change scores indicate that while experimental groups tended to score lower on fear of success after the treatment, control ones tended to score slightly higher.

Since fear of success has been primarily researched with relation to sex differences, it seemed important to include a further analysis which would yield information as to main and interactive effects of sex on this variable. A two-way analysis of variance (group × sex) was then performed. Corresponding experimental and control groups were combined (both GSC, both GRC and both AAG) in order to ensure adequate cell size. The results presented in Table 15 reveal a significant main effect for group and for sex, and a significant interaction of group × sex.

Table 15. Results of analysis of variance for interactive effects of group by sex for fear of success

By Source of variation	Main effects Group Sex SS	DF	2-way interaction Group MS	Sex F	P
Main effects	109.586	3	36.529	28.114	0.000
Group	50.154	2	25.077	19.300	0.000
Sex	60.586	1	60.586	46.629	0.000
2-way interactions	20.533	2	10.266	7.901	0.001
Group—Sex	20.533	2	10.266	7.901	0.001
Explained	130.119	5	26.024	20.029	0.000
Residual	85.755	66	1.299		
Total	215.875	71	3.040		

* Two-way analysis of variance

Examination of group means indicates the main effect for group derived from the tendency of gifted pupils of both sexes who study in special classes to score higher on fear of success than those in regular classes or average-ability underachievers, and for gifted pupils in general to score higher than those of average ability (see Table 16).

Table 16. Means for fear of success by group and sex

	Gifted in special classes M	n	Gifted in regular classes M	n	Average ability M	n
Girls	5.88	8	5.33	12	2.50	10
Boys	3.13	16	2.75	12	2.14	14

The main effect for sex derived from the finding that girls scored higher than boys in all groups, although this difference was strikingly large among the gifted, and only slight among the average-ability underachievers. The significant interaction effect derived from the finding that while the difference between the scores of gifted and average-ability girls was very large, that between gifted and average-ability boys, while in the same direction, was smaller. Interestingly, while the average-ability girls scored only slightly higher than the average-ability boys, gifted girls scored much higher than gifted boys.

4. TREATMENT VARIABLES

The second group of questions related to characteristics of the treatment itself. Three hypotheses were formulated, which related both to expected patterns over the experimental subjects as a whole and to expected differences in the intervention process among gifted as compared with average-ability subjects. The results pertaining to each hypothesis will be presented in turn.

(a) SUCCESS ON TASK

The hypothesis that all experimental groups would achieve a higher rate of 'success on tasks' towards the end of the treatment was confirmed. Table 17 presents the average percentage of success (as a proportion of the number of tasks selected) in each experimental group for the first three sessions as compared with the final three sessions.

Table 17. % of success on tasks selected in late as compared with early sessions, by experimental group

	Research group							
	GSR		GRC		AAG		Total	
	No. successes		Successes		Successes		Successes	
	No. tasks		Tasks		Tasks		Tasks	
	%		%		%		%	
First 3 sessions	27	31	17	24	10	15	54	24
	88		72		67		227	
Last 3 sessions	80	92	81	99	37	95	198	95
	87		82		39		208	

(b) CHOICE OF FOCI

This hypothesis stated that the gifted underachievers would tend to select more foci for each session than would the average-ability underachievers, that their choice of foci would not be restricted to only one of the three possible domains, scholastic, social and behavioural, in each session. This hypothesis was tested in two stages. First an X^2 test of association between group and preference for number of foci per session was computed to test the hypothesis that there would be a significant association between group membership and selection of more or fewer tasks per session.

The results presented as Table 18 do indeed indicate a significant association between group membership and the tendency to choose one, two or three foci at each session. This pattern is further clarified by Table 19, which presents the percentage of choices of one, two or three foci in each group, indicating that gifted pupils chose more treatment foci than average-ability underachievers.

Table 18. X^2 test of association between research group and choice of 1, 2 or 3 foci per pupil per session

| | Research group | | | |
No. of foci chosen	GSC	GRC	AAG	Total
1	11	41	100	152
2	74	63	38	175
3	59	40	6	105
	144	144	144	432

$X^2 = 138.92$
df = 4
sig. at $p < 0.05$

Table 19. % of choices of one, two or three foci by pupils in each experimental group

| | Research group | | |
No. of foci chosen	GSC	GRC	AAG
1	7	28	69
2	51	44	26
3	42	28	5

In addition, a second X^2 test of association was computed to test the hypothesis that the single choices of the average ability would tend to be made in one domain alone—the scholastic domain—while the choices of gifted pupils would tend to be more evenly distributed over the different domains.

Table 20. X^2 test of association between experimental group and number of choices from each behavioural domain

| | Group | | | |
Domain	GSC	GRC	AAG	Total
Scholastic	138	97	130	365
Social	129	123	44	296
Behavioural	73	68	21	162
	340	288	195	823

$X^2 = 52.25$
df = 4
sig. at $p < 0.05$

Table 20 reveals a significant association which confirms the general hypothesis that most of the choices of average-ability underachievers would be from the scholastic domain, while those of the gifted groups would be more evenly distributed over the three domains. It is interesting that while gifted pupils in special classes tended to select learning foci slightly more frequently than social ones, those in regular classes chose social foci more often. Thus the results again indicate that while the patterns among gifted and average-ability pupils differ, so also do those among the two gifted groups.

(c) Reward selection

The final treatment-related hypothesis stated that gifted pupils would be less likely to request rewards contingent on successful completion of tasks than would the average-ability subjects. As indicated in Table 21 there were indeed striking differences between the two ability groups. The percentage of rewards requested by the two gifted groups was very similar, and far lower than that requested by the average-ability group.

Table 21. % of tasks for which a reward was requested, by experimental group

| | GS | GSC | | | GRC | | | AAG | |
No. of rewards		No. of tasks	%	No. of rewards	No. of tasks	%	No. of rewards	No. of tasks	%
60		330	18	60	289	21	106	194	55

5. TEACHER VARIABLES

The third major question raised by this study was concerned with the effect of the teacher on the success of the intervention treatment. As discussed above, four variables were assumed to be related to teachers' expectations:

A—Recognizing the need for change.
B—Expectations from pupil.
C—Expectations from treatment.
D—Acceptance of responsibility.

(a) The relationships between teacher variables and treatment success

In general, it was hypothesized that teacher expectations and the success of the treatment would be positively correlated. As shown in Table 22, this hypothesis was supported. In addition, four specific hypotheses were formulated, each relating to one of the four teacher variables and the success of the treatment.

Table 22. Pearson correlation matrix between variables measuring teachers' expectations
from the treatment and success of treatment (succtreat)

Variable succreat	Succreat	A	B	C	D
succreat	—				
A	0.26***	—			
B	0.68***	0.37***	—		
C	0.67***	0.42***	0.85***	—	
D	0.37***	0.54***	0.49***	0.58***	—

*** Significant at $p \leq 0.008$

In order to test this group of hypotheses it was decided to use non-parametric
methods. These relationships, using X^2 tests of associations, were performed. In
addition, the Fisher's Exact Test was performed in order to describe the degree by
which values of one variable predict or vary with those of another. In order to
examine the relationship between the teachers' variables success of treatment ('succtreat') the teachers' scores (range: 1−100 per cent) were divided into two groups: low
and high scores. Low = 1−70 per cent; high = 71−100 per cent. Similarly, the
children's succtreat scores were also divided into two groups: low = 1−6 per cent;
high = 7−11 per cent.

In order to test the specific relationships, X^2 tests of association were performed.
In addition, the Fisher's Exact Test was performed in order to describe the degree by
which values of one variable predict or vary with those of another. The results
presented in Tables 23−26 indicated significant associations between 'expectations
from pupil' and 'expectations from treatment' and 'treatment success'. However, the
associations between 'treatment success' and 'recognition of need for change' and
'acceptance of responsibility' were not significant. These results indicate that while
the general relationships between teacher and treatment variables were as
hypothesized, these were more strongly confirmed for variables specifically relating
to 'expectation' than they were for non-expectancy variables.

Table 23. X^2 cross-table of 'recognition of change' by 'succtreat'

Recognition of change	Succtreat Low	High	Total
Low	7	7	14
High	5	17	22
Total	12	24	36

$X^2 = 1.77$
$df = 1$
$p = 0.183$
Fisher = 0.28

Table 24. X^2 cross-table of 'expectation from pupil' by 'succtreat'

Expectation from pupil	Succtreat Low	High	Total
Low	6	0	6
High	6	24	30
Total	12	24	36

$X^2 = 11.02$
df = 1
p = 0.000
Fisher = 0.63

Table 25. X^2 cross-table of 'expectation from treatment' by 'succtreat'

Expectation from treatment	Succtreat Low	High	Total
Low	7	2	9
High	5	22	27
Total	12	24	36

$X^2 = 8.17$
df = 1
p = 0.004
Fisher = 0.54

Table 26. X^2 cross-table of 'acceptance of responsibility' by 'succtreat'

Acceptance of responsibility	Succtreat Low	High	Total
Low	9	13	22
High	3	11	14
Total	12	24	36

$X^2 = .72$
df = 1
p = 0.397
Fisher = 0.20

6. SUMMARY OF OUTCOMES

(a) Child variables

The results did not reveal any consistent differences between the pre-intervention characteristics of underachievers in the two ability groups. The picture was rather one that differed slightly from group to group, although the results did indicate that, especially on the educational variables and also on some of the psychological ones, two groups tended to score particularly and consistently low—the experimental groups GRC and AAG. The only clear pre-treatment pattern was revealed for fear of success, where girls scored higher than boys and gifted higher than average-ability underachievers. In contrast, the post-intervention picture revealed that the intervention favourably affected the status of underachievers on the various educational variables studied.

While no such directional hypothesis was formulated for the psychological variables, on the assumption that such measures reflect underlying characteristics resistant to change over the short term, certain interesting patterns emerged. Change scores on most of the variables, with the exception of need achievement, were in fact significant. Striking gains were made mainly by the two originally 'problematic' experimental groups mentioned above. In general, these results indicated that at least some changes, even in psychological characteristics, were effected by the intervention.

(b) Treatment variables

Treatment characteristics yielded the following patterns:

(1)   Rate of success on treatment tasks was higher in later sessions than in earlier ones, in all experimental groups.
(2)   Gifted pupils chose more tasks per session than did average-ability pupils.
(3)   The tasks chosen by average-ability pupils tended to be mostly from a scholastic domain, while those chosen by gifted pupils tended to be more evenly distributed over all domains. In all groups, least tasks were chosen from the behavioural domain.
(4)   Average-ability pupils chose more rewards contingent on successful task completion than did gifted pupils. In addition, the results revealed an interesting pattern whereby average-ability pupils requested successively fewer rewards as the treatment progressed, while gifted ones requested more in later than in earlier sessions.

(c) Teacher variables

Generally a positive relationship between various aspects of teacher expectations and perception and success of the treatment was found. Specifically the results revealed:

(1)   A significant effect of the teacher on success of treatment.
(2)   Correlations between teacher variables and treatment success were positive and significant.
(3)   Further investigation of these relationships in terms of X^2 tests of association indicated significant associations between: 'expectations from pupil' and 'expectations from treatment' and treatment success. However, the associations between treatment success and 'recognition of need for change' and 'acceptance of responsibility' were not significant. These results thus indicated that while the general relationships between teacher and treatment variables were as

hypothesized, these were more strongly confirmed for variables specifically relating to 'expectation' than they were for non-expectancy variables.

In order to test not only the strength but also the nature of these relationships, Pearson Product-Moment Correlation coefficients were computed for each teacher variable. Intercorrelations presented as Table 27 indicate that while all were significant, the highest correlation was found between the variables 'expectations from treatment' and 'expectations from pupil'.

Table 27. Pearson correlation matrix between variables measuring teachers' expectations from treatment

	*A	*B	*C	*D
*A	—			
*B	0.37***	—		
*C	0.42***	0.85***	—	
*D	0.54***	0.49***	0.58***	—

*A = Need for change
 B = Expectation from the pupil
 C = Expectation from the treatment
 D = Acceptance of responsibility
*** Significant at p 0.008

7. CORRELATION BETWEEN SUCCESS OF TREATMENT VARIABLES (SUCCTREAT)

Since I was concerned with establishing the relationship between teachers' expectations and the success of the treatment, it was necessary first to determine whether there is a positively significant correlation between the two variables defined as 'success of treatment'—'mean school grade', and 'success on tasks'. As Pearson correlation computed between these variables was significant (R = 0.42, p 0.008), it was considered valid to combine the change in pre- and post-mean scores on the two success of treatment variables, and a new index, to be called 'succtreat', was created.

References

Altus, W.D. (1948). A college achiever and non-achiever scale for the Minnesota Multiphasic Personality Inventory, *Journal of Applied Psychology*, **32**, 385−97

Atkinson, J.W. (ed.) (1958). *Motives in Fantasy, Action and Society: A Method of Assessment and Study*, New York: Van Nostrand

Atkinson, J.W. and Litwin, G.H. (1966). Achievement motive and test anxiety conceived as motive to approacy success and to avoid failure, in Atkinson, J.W. and Feather, N.T. (eds), *A Theory of Achievement Motivation*, New York: Wiley

Atkinson, J.W. and Raynor, J.O. (1974). *Motivation and Achievement*, Washington, D.C.: Winston and Sons

Bar-Tal, D. and Bar-Zohar, Y. (1977). The relationship between perception of locus of control and academic achievement, *Contemporary Education Psychology*, **2**, 181−99

Baymur, F.B. and Patterson, C.H. (1965). A comparison of three methods of assisting underachieving high school students, in Kornrich, M. (ed.), *Underachievement*, Illinois: Thomas, C. Charles, pp. 501−13

Bem, D.J. (1972). Self-perception theory, in Berkovitz, L. (ed.) *Advances in Experimental Social Psychology*, New York: Academic

Bem, S.L. (1974). The measurement of psychological androgyny, *J. of Consulting and Clinical Psychology*, **42**, 155−62

Burt, C. (1962). *The Gifted Child Yearbook of Education*, London: Evans

Burt, C. (1975). *The Gifted Child*, London: Umbooks, Hodder and Stoughton

Butler, N. (1976). Israel's first experiment in special classes for gifted children within regular schools, in Gibson, J. and Chennels, P. (eds), *Gifted Children: Looking to their Future*, London: Latimer New Dimensions

Butler, N. and Butler, R. (1979). Parents' and children's perceptions of special classes for highly gifted children, in Gallagher, J.J. (ed.) *Gifted Children: Reaching Their Potential*, Jerusalem: Kollek

Butler, R. and Nisan, M. (1975). Who is afraid of success and why? *Journal of Youth and Adolescence*, **4**, 259−70

Butler-Por, N. (1982). The phenomenon and treatment of academic underachievement, in Children of Superior and Average Abilities, unpublished PhD. dissertation, University of Wales, University College, Cardiff

Butler-Por, N. (1983). Giftedness across cultures, in Shore, B.M., Gagne, F., Larivee, S., Tali, R.H. and Tremblay, R.E. (eds), *Face to Face with Giftedness*, The World Council for the Gifted, New York: Trillium Press, pp. 250−70

Butler-Por, N. (1985). Gifted children in three Israeli cultures, *The Psychology of Gifted Children*, Joan Freeman (ed.), Chichester, New York: John Wiley

Carelli, A.O. (1981). Creative dramatics for the gifted: A multi-disciplinary approach, *Roeper Review*, **5**(2), 29-31

Charlton, A.G. (1980)Effects of school-based counselling on locus of control, M.Ed. thesis, University of Wales

Clark, L.N. (1978). Let's make a deal: contingency contracting with adolescents, *American*

Secondary Education, **8**, 12–23

Clizbe, J.A., Kornrich, M. and Reid, M.A. (1980). *Chance for change: Confronting Student Underachievement*, New York: Exposition

Coleman, J.S. (1961). *The Adolescent Society*, New York: Free Press

Coleman, J.S. (1965). The adolescent subculture and academic achievement, in Kornrich, M. (ed.), *Underachievement*, Illinois: Charles C. Thomas

Collins, J.F. (1961). *An interim report of an experimental program with underachievers, A-36.* New York: State Education Department.

Crandall, V.C., Katkovsky, W. and Preston, A. (1965). Children's beliefs in their own control of reinforcement in intellectual-academic achievement situations, *Child Development*, **36**, 91–109

Davis, G.A. and Rimm, S.B. (1985). *Education of the Gifted and Talented*, Englewood Cliffs, New Jersey: Prentice-Hall

Decharmes, R. (1972). Personal causation training in the schools, *Journal of Applied Social Psychology*, 2, 95–113

Delph, J.L. and Martinson, R.A. (1974). *The Gifted and Talented*, Washington D.C.: Office of Education

Diedrich, R.C. and Dye, H.A. (eds) (1972). *Group Procedures: Purposes, Processes and Outcomes*. Boston: Houghton and Mifflin

Erikson, E.H. (1963). *Childhood and Society*, New York: Norton

Fine, B. (1967). *Underachievers: How They Can Be Helped*, New York: Dutton

Fink, M.B. (1962). Self-concept as it relates to academic underachievement, *Journal of Educational Research*, **13**, 57–62

Frankel, E.A. (1960). A comparative study of achieving and underachieving high school boys of high intellectual ability, *Journal of Educational Research*, **53**, 172–80

Freeman, J. (1979). *Gifted Children: Their Identification and Development in a Social Context*, Baltimore: MTP Press, Lancaster and University Park Press

French, E.G. (1958). Development of a measure of complex motivation, in Atkinson, J.W. (ed.), *Motives in Fantasy, Action and Society*, Princeton: Van Nostrand

Gallagher, J.J. (1985). *Teaching The Gifted Child*, 3rd edn, Boston: Allyn & Bacon

Gardner, J. (1961). *Excellence: Can we be Equal and Excellent too?* New York: Harper

Getzels, J.W. and Jackson, P.W. (1962). *Creativity and Intelligence*, New York: John Wiley

Glasser, W. (1965). *Reality Therapy*, New York: Harper & Row

Glasser, W. (1969). *Schools Without Failure*, New York: Harper & Row

Goodlad, J. (1970). The reconstruction of teacher education, *Teachers' Record* (Columbia University) **72**, 1

Hargreaves Report (1984). *Improving Secondary Schools*, London: Inner London Education Authority

Heider, F. (1965). *The Psychology of Interpersonal Relations*, New York: John Wiley

Hitchfield, E.M. (1973). *In Search of Promise*, London: Longman

Horner, M.S. (1968). Sex differences in achievement and performance in competitive and non-competitive situations, Ph.D. dissertation, University of Michigan

Hudson, L. (1966). *Contrary Imagination*, New York: Schocken

Karnes, M.B. (1963). The efficacy of two organizational plans for underachieving gifted children, *Exceptional Children*, **29**, 430–46

Kelley, H.H. (1967). Attribution theory in social psychology, in Levine, E. (ed.), *Nebraska Symposium on Motivation*, Lincoln: University of Nebraska

Kellmer-Pringle, M.L. (1970). *Able Misfits*, London: Longman

Khatena, J. (1982). *Educational Psychology of the Gifted*, New York: John Wiley

Kornrich, M. (ed.) (1965). *Underachievement*, Illinois: Charles C. Thomas

Kowitz, G.T. (1965). An analysis of underachievement, in Kornrich, M. (ed.) *Underachievement*, Illinois: Charles C. Thomas

Lawrence, D. (1973). *Improved Reading Through Counselling*, London: Wardlock

Levy, A. and Chen, N. (1971). *Achievement Series Chinuch Hayesodi*, Jerusalem: Israeli Ministry of Education

Lewin, K. (1948). Conduct, knowledge and acceptance of new values, in *Resolving Social Conflicts*, New York: Harper

Maslow, A.H. (1954). *Motivation and Personality*, New York: Harper

McClelland, D.C., Atkinson, J.W., Clark, R.A., and Lowell, E.L. (1953). *The Achievement Motive*, New York: Appleton-Century-Croft

McClelland, D.C. (1958). The importance of early learning in the formation of motives, in Atkinson, J.W. (ed.), *Motives in Fantasy, Action and Society*, Princeton: Van Nostrand

McClinton, C.G. and Avermaet, G.V. (1975). The effects of manipulating feedback upon children's motives and performance, *Behavioural Science*, **20**, 101–16

McHolland, J.D. (1971). *Human Potential Seminars. An Approach to Turning on the Gifted Underachiever*, paper presented at the American Association of School Administrators Convention in Atlantic City

Milgram, R., Milgram, N. and Landau, E. (1974). *Identification of Gifted Children in Israel*, Tel-Aviv: Tel-Aviv University

Mitchell, K.K. and Piatkowska, O.E. (1974). Characteristics associated with under-achievement: Targets for treatment, *Australian Journal of Education*, **4**, 19–41

Moulin, E.K. (1970). The effects of client-centred group counseling using play media on the intelligence, achievement and psycholinguistic abilities of underachieving primary school children, *Elementary School Guidance and Counseling*, **5**, 85–95

Moulton, A. (1958). Measurement and scoring of fear of failure, in Atkinson, J.W. (ed.) *Motives in Fantasy, Action and Society*, New York: Van Nostrand

Nevo, B., Sefer, M., Ramraz, R. (1982). *Gender Differences in Cognitive Functioning among University Applicants in Israel*, a paper delivered at the International Interdisciplinary Congress on Women, University of Haifa

Newsom, J. (1963). *Half Our Future*, London H.M.S.O.

Nisan, M. and Butler R. (1979). The influence of receiving evaluation on intrinsic motivation, in Lust, U. and Nisan, M. (eds), *Psychology in Teaching*, Jerusalem: Otzar Hamoreh.

Ohlsen, M.M. and Proff, F.C. (1960). The extent to which group counselling improves the academic and personal adjustment of the underachieving gifted adolescents, Urbana: University of Illinois

Paschal, A.S. (1961). Early correction reading program in San Diego schools. *Curriculum Digest*, San Diego schools in Action, 22

Passow, A.H. (1980). *There Is Gold In Them Thar Hills*, paper presented at the Fourth Biennial National Conference on Disadvantaged Gifted Children, New York: Columbia University, Teachers College

Perkins, J.A. and Wicas, E.A. (1963). Group counseling bright underachievers and their mothers, *Journal of Counseling Psychology*, **13**, 273–8

Piaget, J. and Inhelder, B. (1958). *The Growth of Logical Thinking*, London: Routledge

Pilling, D. and Pringle, M. (1978). *Controversial Issues in Child Development*, London: Paul Elek

Plowden, Lady Bridget *et al.* (1967). *Children and Their Primary Schools*, London: H.M.S.O.

Premack, D. (1959). Reinforcement theory, in Levine, D. (ed.), *Nebraska Symposium on Motivation*, Nebraska University

Raph, J.B., Goldberg, M.L. and Passow, A.H. (1966). *Bright Underachievers*, New York: Teachers College

Rawls, J. (1971). *A Theory of Justice*, Cambridge, Mass.: Harvard University Press

Reis, S.M. and Renzulli, J.S. (1982). A case for broadened conception of giftedness, *Phi Delta Kappa*, **63**, 619–20

Richmond Plan: evaluation of the program (1968). *Office of Education Br*, **5**, Washington D.C.: Stanford Research

Rimm, S.B. (1984). *Underachievement. GICT*, A magazine for parents and teachers of gifted, creative and talented children, 26–9

Rogers, C.R. (1969). The process of the encounter group, *Psychology Today*, **3**, 201–48

Rogers, C.R. (1970). *Encounter Groups*, Harmondsworth: Penguin

Rosenthal, R. and Jacobson, L. (1968). *Pygmalion in the Classroom: Teacher Expectations and Pupil's Intellectual Development*, New York: Holt, Rinehart & Winston

Roth, R.N. and Meyersberg, H.A. (1963). The non-achievement syndrome, *Personnel and Guidance Journal*, **41**, 40–535

Rotter, J.B. (1954). *Social Learning and Clinical Psychology*, New York: Prentice-Hall

Rotter, J.B. (1966). Generalized expectancies for internal versus external control of reinforcement, *Psychological Monographs*, **80**

Rutter, M., Maughan, B., Mortimer, P. and Ouston, J. (1979). *Fifteen Thousand Hours*, Somerset: Open Books

Sarason, I.G. (1980) (Ed.) Test Anxiety: Theory, Research and Application. Hillsdale, N.J.: Erlbaum.

Schneider, R.W. (1977). Need affiliation and sex as modifiers of related need for achievement and academic performance, *Journal of Social Psychology*, **15**, 269–77

Shaw, M.C. (1961). Need achievement scales as predictors of academic success, *Journal of Educational Psychology*, **52**, 282–5

Shaw, M.C. and Alves, G.J. (1963). The self-concept of bright academic underachievers, *The Personnel and Guidance Journal*, **4**, 401–3

Shaw, M.C. and Black, M.D. (1960). The reaction to frustration of bright high school underachievers, *California Journal of Educational Research*, **11**, 120–4

Shaw, M.C. and Grubb, J. (1958). Hostility and able high school underachievers, *Journal of Counseling Psychology*, **5**, 263–6

Shaw, M.C. and McCuen, J.T. (1960). The onset of academic underachievement in bright children, *Journal of Educational Psychology*, **51**, 102–8

Simon, R.H. and Bibb, J.J. (1974). Achievement motivation, test anxiety and underachievement in the elementary school, *Journal of Educational Research*, **67**, 366–9

Tannenbaum, A. (1962). *Adolescent Attitudes Toward Academic Brilliance*, New York: Teachers' College Press

Tannenbaum, A. (1984). *Gifted Children*, New York: Macmillan

Tempest, N.R. (1974). *Teaching Clever Children*, London: Routledge, Kegan & Paul

Terman, L.M. and Oden, M.H. (1947). *Genetic Studies of Genius*, **4**, California: Stanford University Press

Thelen, H.A. (1972). Purpose and process in groups, in Diedrich, R.C. and Dye, H.A. (eds), *Group Procedures: Purposes, Processes and Outcomes*, Boston: Houghton Mifflin

Thomas Committee Report (1984). *Improving Primary Schools*, London: Thomas N., Chairman I.L.E.A. Report

Torrance, E.P. (1972). *Gifted Children in the Classroom*, New York: Macmillan

Waddington, M. and O'Brien, G. (1979) *Promise Unfolding*, London: NAGC

Weiner, B. (1974). *Achievement Motivation and Attribution Theory*, Morristown, New Jersey: General Learning Press

Wellington, C.B. and Wellington, J. (1963). *The Underachiever: Challenges and Guidelines*, Chicago: Rand McNally

White, B.L. (1985). The origins of competence, in Shore, B.M., Gayne, S.L., Tali, R.H., Tremblay, R.E. (Eds.) *Face to Face with Giftedness*, New York: Trillium Press

White, R.W. (1959). Motivation reconsidered: The concept of competence, *Psychological Review*, **66**, 297–333

Whitmore, J.R. (1980). *Giftedness, Conflict and Underachievement*, Boston: Allyn and Bacon

Winborn, B. and Schmidt, L.G. (1962). Effectiveness of short-term group counselling upon the academic achievement of potentially superior but underachieving college freshmen, *Journal of Educational Research*, **55**, 169–73

Zilli, M.G. (1971). Reasons why gifted adolescents underachieve and some of the implications of guidance and counselling to this problem, *The gifted Child Quarterly*, **15**, 279−92

Ziv, A. and Shechori, C. (1968). The efficacy of group treatment for parents of problem children, *Megamot*, **15**, 112−395

Ziv, A. (1975). Self-image of underachieving children, *Studies of Education*, **9**, 91−8

Bibliography

Applebaum, M.J. (1961). A special guidance program for gifted underachievers of the tenth grade, *Bulletin of the National Association of Secondary School Principles*, **45**, 20−33

Argyris, C. (1964). T-groups for organizational effectiveness, *Harvard Business Review*, **42** 60−74

Armstrong, M.E. (1955). A comparison of interests and social adjustment of underachievers and normal achievers at the secondary school level, *Dissertation Abstract*, **15**(12), 1349−50

Arndt, J.R. (1971). *Underachievement: A general Overview*, U.S. Department of Health Education and Welfare: National Institute of Education

Atkinson, J.W. (1957). Motivational determinants of risk-taking behaviour, *Psychological Review*, **64**, 359−72

Bachtold, L.M. (1969). Personality differences among high-ability underachievers, *Journal of Educational Research*, **63**, 16−18

Banner, C.N. (1979). Child-rearing attitudes of mothers of under-average and overachieving children, *British Journal of Educational Psychology*, **49**, 150−5

Blackman, G.J. (1955). A clinical study of the personal structures and adjustments of pupils underachieving and overachieving in reading, *Dissertation Abstracts*, **15**, 1199−200

Blalock, H.M., Jr (1972). *Social Statistics*, New York: McGraw-Hill

Blumberg, A. and Golembiewski, R.T. (1976). *Learning and Change in Groups*, Harmondsworth: Penguin

Bricklin, B. and Bricklin, P.M. (1967). *Bright Child, Poor Grades: The Psychology of Underachievement*, New York: Delacorte

Bridges, S.A. (ed.) (1969). *Gifted Children and the Brentwood Experiment*, London: Pitman

Bridges, S.A. (1975). *The Gifted Children and the Millfield Experiment*, London: Pitman

Bridgman, D.S. (1960). Where the loss of talent occurs and why, in *The Search for Talent*, New York: College Entrance Board

Bronfenbrenner, U. (1960). Freudian theories of identification and their derivations, *Child Development*, **31**, 15−40

Brown, D.R. (1962).Personality, college environment and academic productivity, in Sanford, N.C. (ed.), *The American College*, New York: Wiley

Bruner, J.S. and Caron, A.J. (1959). *Cognition, Anxiety and Achievement in the Pre-adolescent*, Cambridge, Mass: Harvard University Press.

Caldwell, E. (1962). *Short Term Effect of Intrinsic Vocational Counseling upon Talented Students with Inferior School Marks*, Tallahassee: State Department of Education

Calhoun, S.R. (1956). The effect of counseling on a group of eighth grade underachievers, *Dissertation Abstract*, **16**, 1397−8

Campbell, J.P. (1972). Laboratory education: Research results and research needs, in Diedrich, R.C. and Dye, H.A. (eds) *Group Procedures: Purposes, Processes and Outcomes*, Boston: Houghton-Mifflin

Campbell, P.B. (1967). School and self-concept, *Educational Leadership*, **24**, 510−15

Caplan, G. (1959). *Concepts of Mental Health and Consultation*, Washington, D.C.: Department of Health, Education and Welfare

Caron, A.J. (1965). Variables on knowledge seeking behaviour, in Aschner, M.J. and Bish, C.E. (eds), *Productive Thinking in Education*, Washington, D.C.: National Education Association

Carter, H.D. (1961). Overachievers and underachievers in the junior high school, *California Journal of Education Research*, **12**, 51−6

Chance, J.E. (1965). Independence training and first graders' achievement, in Kornrich, M.C. (ed.), *Underachievement*, Illinois: Charles C. Thomas

Chandall, V.J. *et al.* (1965). Children's beliefs in their own control of reinforcement in intellectual-academic achievement situations, *Child Development*, **36**, 91−109

Chansky, N.M. (1965). Perceptual training with elementary school underachievers, in Kornrich, M. (ed.), *Underachievement*, Illinois: Charles C. Thomas

Chevraut, H.L. (1975). Use of behaviour modification concepts with adolescent under-achievers to improve school achievement through attitude change, *Dissertation Abstracts International*, **36**(*4-B*), 1940−1

Chopra, S.L. (1967). A comparative study of achieving and underachieving students of high intellectual ability, *Exceptional Children*, **33**, 9, 631−4

Christie, J.R. (1949). The effects of frustration on rigidity in problem solution, Ph.D. dissertation, University of California

Clark, K.B. (1956). The most valuable hidden reserve, *College Education Review*, **29**, 23−6

Clarks, E.C. (1962). Factors relating to underachievement, *School and Community*, **49**, 22−3

Combs, C.F. (1964). Perception and self-scholastic underachievement in the academically capable, *Personnel and Guidance Journal*, **34**, 47−51

Cooley, C.H. (1909). *Social Organization: A study of the Larger Mind*, New York: Schocken

Coopersmith, S. (1967). *The Antecedents of Self-Esteem*, San Francisco: Freeman

Cornish, R.L. (1967). Studies of gifted children completed by students at the University of Kansas, *Kansas Studies in Education*, **17**

Cronbach, L.J. (1975). Beyond the two disciplines of scientific psychology, *American Psychologist*, **30**, 116−26

Crow, L.D. and Crow, A. (1963). *Educating the Academically Able*, New York: McKay

Curry, R.L. (1962). The effect of socioeconomic status on the scholastic achievement of sixth-grade children, *British Journal of Educational Psychology*, **32**, 46−9

Darley, J.G. (1937). Scholastic achievement and measured maladjustment, *Journal of Applied Psychology*, **21**, 485−93

Davids, A. and Hainsworth, P.K. (1967). Maternal attitudes about family life and child rearing as allowed by mothers and perceived by their underachieving and high achieving sons, *Journal Consultant Psychology*, **31**, 29−37

Davidson, H.H. and Long, G. (1960). Children's perceptions of their teacher's feelings toward them, related to self-perception, school achievement and behaviour, *Journal of Experimental Education*, **29**, 107−18

Dowd, R.J. (1952). Underachieving students of high capacity, *Journal of Higher Education*, **23**, 327−30

Drews, E.M. and Teahan, J.E. (1957). Parental attitude and academic achievers, *Journal of Clinical Psychology*, **13**, 328−32

Duff, O.L. and Siegal, L. (1960). Biographical factors associated with academic over and underachievement, *Journal of Educational Psychology*, **51**, 43−6

Duncan, D.R. (1962). *Effects of Required Group Counseling with College Students in Academic Difficulty*, Ph.D. dissertation, University of Florida

Edelston, H. (1950). Educational failure with high intelligence quotient; A clinical study, *Journal of Genetic Psychology*, **77**, 85−116

Erhard, H. (1972). *Environmental Factors, Ability and Underachievement in Gifted Children*, M.A. thesis, University of Tel-Aviv

Fitzpatrick, J.L. (1978). Academic underachievement, other directions and attitudes toward women's roles in bright adolescent females, *Journal of Educational Psychology*, **70**, 645−50

Fleming, E. and Auttonen, R. (1971). *Teacher Expectancy as related to the Academic and Personal Growth of Primary School Children*, monograph of the Society for Research in Child Development, 145

Fliegler, L.A. (1957). Understanding the underachieving gifted child, *Psychological Reports*, **3**, 533−6

Ford, T.R. (1956). Social factors affecting academic performance: future evidence, *School Review*, **4**, 415−22

French, E.G. (1955). Some characteristics of achievement motivation, *Journal of Experimental Psychology*, **50**, 232-6

Gallagher, J.J. (1958). Peer acceptance of highly gifted children, *Elementary School Journal*, **58**, 465−70

Gallagher, J.J. (1966). *Research Summary on Gifted Education*, Springfield: Department of Programmes Planning for the Gifted

Goldberg, M.L. (1965) Three experimental studies to improve the academic performance of high school underachievers, in Kornrich, M. (ed.), *Underachievement*, Illinois: Charles C. Thomas

Goldburgh, S.J. and Penney, J.F. (1965). A note on counselling underachieving college students, in Kornrich, M. (ed.) *Underachievement*, Illinois: Charles C. Thomas

Gold, M.J. (1965). *Education of the Intellectually Gifted*, Columbus: Charles E. Merkil

Goodlad, J.S. (1964).Understanding the self in the school setting, *Childhool Education*, **41**, 9−14

Gowan, J.C. (1957). Dynamics of the underachievement of gifted students, *Exceptional Children*, **24**, 98-102

Gurman, A.S. (1970). The role of the family in underachievement, *Journal of School Psychology*, **8**, 48−53

Haggard, E.A. (1957). Socialization, personality and academic achievement in gifted children, *School Review*, **65**, 388−414

Hall, W.E. and Gaeddert, W. (1960). Social skills and their relationships to scholastic achievement, *Journal of Genetic Psychology*, **96**, 269−73

Heilbrun, A.B. and Walters, D.B. (1968). Underachievers as related to perceived maternal child rearing and academic conditions of reinforcement, *Child Development*, **39**, 913−21

Heinemann, A. (1977). *Star Power: Providing for the Gifted and Talented: Underachievers Among the Gifted and Talented*, Austin: Education Service

Helmreich, R. (1972). Stress, self-esteem and attitudes, in King, B.T. and McGinnies, E. (eds), *Attitudes, Conflict and Social Change*, London: Academic

Hildreth, G.H. (1966). *Introduction to the Gifted*, New York: McGraw-Hill

Hilliard, T. and Roth, R.M. (1969). Maternal attitudes and the non-achievement syndrome, *Personnel and Guidance Journal*, **47**, 424−8

Holmes, F.B. (1962). A study of the psychological, emotional and intellectual factors associated with academic underachievement, *Independent School Bulletin* 1, 54−9

Kehas, C.D. (1963). *Underachievement as a Function of Self-Concept*, paper presented at the American Personnel and Guidance Association, Washington, D.C.

Leibman, O.B. (1954). The relationship of personal and social adjustment to academic achievement in the elementary school, *Dissertation Abstracts*, **14**, 67

Mallinson, T.J. (1964). *A comparative study of four types of treatment in improving adjustment and school achievement of gifted underachievers: A follow-up study*, Toronto Board of Education (Microfilm), Ontario: Canada Research Department

Marx, G.L. (1959). A comparison of the effectiveness of two methods of counseling with academic underachievers, *Dissertation Abstracts*, **20**(6), 2144−5

McGowan, R.J. (1968). Group counseling with underachievers and their parents, *School Counselor*, **16**, 30−5

Merick, R.D. and Haight, D.A. (1972). Growth groups: an encounter with underachievers, *School Counselor*, **20**, 115−21

Middleton, G. and Guthrie, G.M. (1959). Personality syndromes and academic achievement, *Journal of Educational Psychology* 50, 66–9

Miller, V.V. (1961). *The Early Identification and Treatment of Underachieving Primary School Pupils*, Evanston: Community Consolidated Schools

Mitchell, B. (1963). *The Underachiever: A new Approach*, New York: Brace and World

Morrow, W.R. and Wilson, R.C. (1961). The self-reported personal and social adjustment of bright achieving and underachieving high school boys, *Journal of Psychological Psychiatry*, 2, 203–9

Motto, J.J. (1959). A reply to Drasgow on underachievers, *Journal of Counseling Psychology*, 6, 245–7

Norfleet, M.A. (1968). Characteristics of achieving and underachieving high ability women, *Personnel and Guidance Journal*, 46, 976–80

Norman, R.D. (1966). The interpersonal values of parents of achieving and non-achieving gifted children, *Journal of Psychology*, 64, 49–57

Oden, M.H. (1968). The fulfilment of promise: 40 years follow-up of Terman's gifted group, *Genetic Psychology Monograph* 77

O'Shea, A. (1970). Low achievement syndrome among bright junior high school boys, *Journal of Educational Research*, 63, 257–62

Passow, A.H. and Goldberg, M. (1962). The talent youth project, *Exceptional Children* 28, 223–31

Pentecoste, J.G. (1975). Effects of small group counseling on cognitive growth of bright underachievers in an atypical educational situation, *Education*, 96, 89–93

Perkins, J.A. and Wicas, E.A. (1963). Group counseling bright underachievers and their mothers, *Journal of Counseling Psychology*, 13, 273–8

Peterson, J. (1963). The researcher and the underachievers, *Phi Delta Kappa*, 44, 378–9

Purkey, W.W. 1968). *Project Self Discovery: Its Effects on Bright Underachievers at Nine Florida High Schools*. Paper presented at annual meeting of American Educational Research Association, Chicago

Shaver, J.P. (1971). The effectiveness of tutoring underachievers in reading and writing, *Journal of Educational Research*, 65, 107–12

Shaw, M.C. (1964a). Note on parent attitudes towards independence training and academic achievement of their children, *Journal of Educational Psychology*, 55, 371–4

Shaw, M.C. (1964b). Definition and identification of academic underachievers, in French, L. (ed.), *Educating the Gifted*, New York: Holt, Rinehart & Winston

Strang, R. (1964). Prevention and correction of underachievement, in Robinson, A. (ed.), *Meeting Individual Differences in Reading*, Chicago: University of Chicago

Sucher, F. (1976). *Factors Contributing to Misbehaviour and Underachievement Among Elementary School Boys*, paper presented at the annual meeting of the International Reading Association, Southern Regional Conference, Florida

Thomas, S.B. (1973). Neglecting the gifted causes them to hide their talents, *Gifted Child Quarterly*, 17, 193–7

Thompson, M.E. (1976). *Distinctive Characteristics of Over and Underachieving Students: A Synthesis of the Research Literature*, U.S. Department of Health and Welfare: National Institute of Education

Thorndike, R.L. (1963). *The Concept of Over and Underachievement*, New York: Teachers' College Press

Author Index

Subject Index